WORDS' WORTH

WORDS' WORTH

What the Poet Does

Claudia Brodsky

BLOOMSBURY ACADEMIC
NEW YORK • LONDON • OXFORD • NEW DELHI • SYDNEY

BLOOMSBURY ACADEMIC
Bloomsbury Publishing Inc
1385 Broadway, New York, NY 10018, USA
50 Bedford Square, London, WC1B 3DP, UK

BLOOMSBURY, BLOOMSBURY ACADEMIC and the Diana logo are
trademarks of Bloomsbury Publishing Plc

First published in the United States of America 2020

Cover design by Eleanor Rose
Cover image: Detail from J. M. W. Turner, *The Red Rigi* 1842, watercolour, wash
and gouache with some scratching out, 30.5 × 45.8 cm (sheet), Wilton 1525,
National Gallery of Victoria, Melbourne, Felton Bequest, 1947 (1704–4)

Bloomsbury Publishing Inc does not have any control over, or responsibility
for, any third-party websites referred to or in this book. All internet
addresses given in this book were correct at the time of going
to press. The author and publisher regret any inconvenience
caused if addresses have changed or sites have ceased to
exist, but can accept no responsibility for any such changes.

Library of Congress Cataloging-in-Publication Data
Names: Brodsky, Claudia, 1955– author.
Title: Words' worth : what the poet does / Claudia Brodsky.
Description: New York : Bloomsbury Academic, 2020. | Includes bibliographical
references and index. | Summary: "Gives students and scholars a new way to
approach the theory and interpretation of poetry and indeed modern
literature"—Provided by publisher.
Identifiers: LCCN 2020009227 | ISBN 9781501364532 (hardback) |
ISBN 9781501364525 (paperback) | ISBN 9781501364556 (pdf) |
ISBN 9781501364549 (ebook)
Subjects: LCSH: Wordsworth, William, 1770-1850—Knowledge–Poetry. |
Poetics. | Poetry—History and criticism—Theory, etc.
Classification: LCC PR5892.P63 B76 2020 | DDC 821/.7—dc23
LC record available at https://lccn.loc.gov/2020009227

ISBN: HB: 978-1-5013-6453-2
       PB: 978-1-5013-6452-5
       ePDF: 978-1-5013-6455-6
       eBook: 978-1-5013-6454-9

Typeset by RefineCatch Limited, Bungay, Suffolk

To find out more about our authors and books visit www.bloomsbury.com
and sign up for our newsletters.

For Chloe and Rebecca

*Toni Morrison, fast friend, constant confidante
in the moral life of words, in Memoriam*

CONTENTS

Part III
Necessary Poetics: Theory of the Real

Acknowledgments

I would like to thank a number of people who, in different, direct and indirect ways, contributed to the progress of this work. Few things matter as much to what we do as our experience of others who take what they do seriously, and nothing can replace the seriousness of commitment to the fundamental importance of Wordsworth's poetics, and of Romanticism in general that, in my experience, united such divergent critics as Geoffrey Hartman, Paul de Man, and Harold Bloom. It was my great fortune to have been able to study with them all, without prejudice to any. Next I would like to thank Alexander Regier who, with his co-editor, Stefan Uhlig, invited me to commit an early version of the following argument concerning poetic action to paper. Sometimes we recognize the workings of an essential dynamic so clearly that we assume others must, and, neglecting to do what we deem unnecessary, fail to articulate and so expose what we see to further reflection and development. It is fair to say that, without the acknowledgment and kind urging of Alexander Regier in particular, that first articulation and this current development and extension of it, in its direct relation to the long-term project on Kant I was completing concurrently, would not have taken place to begin with.

Next I would like to thank those understanding souls who not only accepted but respected my deep-seated occupation with this project. These include Chloe Anna Brooks, Angèle Bixel, Madeleine Gabourin, Lucie Bixel, Dolores Bacon, Emily Jayne Duckworth, John Park, and Toni Morrison. I would also like to thank the members of the Princeton University Committee on Research in the Humanities and Social Sciences for their financial support of my research at the Jerwood Centre Manuscript Library of the Wordsworth Trust in Grasmere, as well as the devoted guides and librarians of the entire Wordsworth Collection.

Finally, I cannot sufficiently thank Sara Bryant, whose tireless, gimlet-eyed efforts have aided every page herein, and my exceptional editor at Bloomsbury, Haaris Naqvi, the most effective, comprehending, and responsible editor I know. Our profession would be strengthened by more professionals of his character and caliber, and I consider myself lucky to have had the benefit, not only of his editorial confidence and advice, but, moreover, of his discerning intellect, foresight and long view.

Part I

Language Theory and Poetics

Chapter 1

Wordsworth and the "Material Difference" of the "Real Language of Men"

Wordsworth's "Preface to *Lyrical Ballads*" opens with the poet's frank acknowledgement of the immediate challenge his poems pose to their comprehension by the reading public: that of being recognized and read as works of poetry to begin with. The public may well have difficulty conceiving as poetic, the poet readily concedes, "poems so materially different from those upon which general approbation is at present bestowed."[1] As the reader of the "Preface" soon discovers, that first admitted obstacle intrinsically harbors another, a kind of ineluctable double that at once contradicts and follows from it, negates yet also, in circular manner, creates it: that of presenting no obstacle to comprehension at all. The problem with these poems is that they pose no "problem"—no abstruse semantic or recondite technical impediment to their comprehension—other than that of posing no problem, no calculated opacity of form or lexical divergence from discursive norms. For the mark of distinction constituting their "material differen[ce]" from other poetry is, specifically, their lack of difference from other uses of language in currency. Thus what appears at first an infinitely regressive logical problem—the problem of there being no problem, i.e., of an "*a*" identical with "*not-a*," or self-contradiction—turns out to be a specifically linguistic one, i.e., how it is, or within what frame of meaning, we understand the specifically poetic significance of terms whose usage is precisely *not* "materially different" from, but, rather, legibly self-identical with the practical norm.

1. William Wordsworth, *The Prose Works of William Wordsworth*, 3 vols., ed. W. J. B. Owen and Jane Worthington Smyser (Oxford: Oxford University Press, 1994), I: 121. All subsequent citations from Wordsworth's prose will be from this edition, which will be referenced with volume and page no. as Owen and Smyser.

The difficulty of identifying the presence of difference in its absence, where none meets the eye, is, the poet realizes, the immediate quandary his contemporary reader faces. Over two centuries of contemporaries (readers co-present with Wordsworth's words) later, that situation remains much the same. Together with the beginnings of *The Prelude*— the "introductory" work whose composition and revision would extend over the entire course of Wordsworth's life—and the other "early" works written during the same "time" that Kant, writing in another introductory context, defined, in unlimited theoretical terms, as "the actual time of critique,"[2] the *Lyrical Ballads* hardly distinguish themselves from works of prose in either vocabulary or subject matter—a distinction that proves no less difficult for the poet himself to make, as we shall see. Yet the "one mark of difference" that "will be found" in the poems by any "reader," Wordsworth contends, and that, in addition, defines, in his general theoretical view, "any poem worthy of the name," is the "worthy purpose" "that each of them has."[3] Still, while declaring and defending throughout the "Preface to *Lyrical Ballads*" the common language his lyrics share with that of ordinary speech, nowhere in the "Preface" does Wordsworth define, by contrast, what that sole distinguishing property, or "worthy purpose," might be.

This study asks whether the purposeful use of commonplace language— the negative condition, in that it appears non-poetic, which, according to Wordsworth, constitutes the "material differen[ce]" of his poems—and the unspecified "worthy purpose" that, on his view, "any poem worthy of the

2. "Our time is the actual time of critique" ("Unsere Zeitalter ist die eigentliche Zeitalter der Kritik"): this extraordinary pronouncement by Kant, made in a note to the "Preface" to the first ("A") edition of his *Critique of Pure Reason* (1781), not only inaugurates the concept of "critique" itself but defines critique as the ability to think theoretically, i.e., guided by "questions" rather than presumptions, at any time, and, in so doing, define the presence ("is") of "our" "actual time." Defining his "time," while famously demonstrating our inherent inability, as temporal sentient beings, positively to define time itself, Kant's analogous defense of the "positive [moral] purpose" of his own "negative," "critical" project occurs in the extensive, historically and theoretically explanatory "Preface" to its second ("B") edition (1787). See Immanuel Kant, *Werkausgabe*, XII vol., ed. Wilhelm Weischedel (Frankfurt: Suhrkamp, 1974), *Kritik der reinen Vernunft* (hereafter *KrV*) A XI, III: 13; B XXIV–XXV, III: 29–30,. All citations from Kant will be from this edition of his collected works. All translations from the German are my own.

3. Owen and Smyser, I: 121.

name" serves, may indeed be, or, in the process of reading, become, one and the same. In short, the following analysis investigates whether the "purpose" of Wordsworth's "Preface," like that of the poems themselves, is not only to redefine the language the reading public considers "poetic" but to demonstrate that, at its most "worthy" of being read, that language is indistinguishable from what he calls "the language of men."[4]

The negation of any essential stylistic difference between poetry and prose that made the "Preface" appear as heterodox as the *Ballads* themselves has made it, in retrospect, one of the founding essays of modern poetics, definitive not only of Wordsworth's own turn-of-the-century poetic practice but the future of all English-language and related Indo-European-language poetry as well. It is no exaggeration to say that, despite differences in subject matter, authorial diction and independence from or adherence to traditional forms of versification, modern poetry after Wordsworth departs from the premise, asserted in the "Preface," that poetry itself is most effectively "poetic" when composed in the language of "prose."

Still, considered more closely, the undoing of the distinction between poetic and prosaic languages at which Wordsworth, writing both as individual practitioner and general theorist of the poetic, aims, must depend on a larger conception of language capable of uniting them. Like the other founding thinkers of modernity, as different as Descartes from Marx, whose shared understanding of the inimitable capacities of human language constitutes the essential, common condition of their work, Wordsworth's conception of language bears no resemblance to that of predetermined and thus inherently predictable "languages" or language "mechanics" (be they artificial or "natural" and species-specific in origin, i.e., the result of externally programmed or genetically transmitted coding[5]), but, rather, the experiential—which is to say, perceptible, affecting, and

---

4. Owen and Smyser, I: 131.

5. Cf. n. 5, Chap. 2, for Wordsworth's Rousseauian critique, already issued in the 1798 "Advertisement" to *Lyrical Ballads*, of "pre-established codes of decision" regarding what constitutes the "'poetic'" and "culture" in general: prescriptions for self-confirming social stratification enforced, as he writes in the "Appendix" to the "Preface" and later "Essay, Supplementary to the Preface" (1815), through their "mechanical" repetition and transmission by "the ruling intellects of the time," the same poetasters who failed to recognize "the mighty genius of Shakespeare" ("Advertisement" of *Lyrical Ballads*, Owen and Smyser, I: 116; "Appendix" to the "Preface", Owen and Smyser, I: 160; "Essay, Supplementary to the Preface," Owen and Smyser, III: 68).

cognizing; demarcating, differentiating, and delineating; graphic, scenographic and memorializing—"real language of men," or as he later defines this in active *adverbial* terms, "the language really spoken by men."[6] Wordsworth is no philosopher nor did he desire or pretend to be; unlike Coleridge (and despite remarkable similarities between his and Kant's understanding of the sublime), he professed no interest in contemporary empirical or idealist thought. Nor did he wish to develop an observational anthropology of which "man" would be the object. Aiming instead to explain an activity as old as human subjects—the specifically human, pragmatically gratuitous act of poetry-making or *poiesis*—Wordsworth reflected instead upon the interactive medium that all persons[7] share: "language," before its usage became defined as valuable in direct proportion to its display of superfluous ornament, divided into poetic and prosaic, and socially stratified into cultural classes of high and low.

Wordsworth's "language of men" is instead what it says: that language at once belonging to and defining human beings alone, not as some innate substance or quality let alone infantilizing, "mimetic" copy machine, they are dreamed to possess, but in their active use, interaction with, and experience of it. The "language really used by men" that Wordsworth conceives is thus coextensive not only with a general conception of poetry but with that of its own, necessarily common origin *among human subjects,* and the "worthy purpose" of that originally common, inherently social language, one might say, would be likewise that of poetry itself: for Wordsworth, as we shall see, the dynamic articulation of the "complex" relations among action, feeling and knowledge occurring within any individual human being, externalized by means of representation for communication among human beings. Before directly examining the simultaneous representation *and* re-enactment of this complexity in the poetry, we would do well to follow the poet and examine his exacting description of the nexus of language and experience in the "Preface" first. For, as Wordsworth most powerfully states toward the close of that expository work, it is the purpose of his own poetry no less than theory of "real language" to "assist the Reader in perceiving" one all-pervasive, moral and social fact: that "the powers of language are not so limited as [one] may suppose."[8]

6. Owen and Smyser, I: 134.

7. This work understands all persons to be included in Wordsworth's designation of men, which we take to be the contemporary equivalent of Kant's "Menschen," collective pronoun, "wir" and neutral third-person pronoun, "man," which is synonymous with the English "one," and Romance language "se" or "si."

8. Owen and Smyser, I: 157.

Chapter 2

A "Complex Scene"

Wordsworth describes the "sublime notion of Poetry which [he has] attempted to convey" in the "Preface" as follows:

> What then does the Poet? He considers man and the objects that surround him as acting and re-acting upon each other, so as to produce an infinite complexity of pain and pleasure; he considers man in his own nature and in his ordinary life as contemplating this with a certain quantity of immediate knowledge, with certain convictions, intuitions, and deductions, which from habit acquire the quality of intuitions; he considers him as looking upon this complex scene of ideas and sensations, and finding everywhere objects that immediately excite in him sympathies which, from the necessities of his nature, are accompanied by an over-balance of enjoyment.[1]

The "complex scene" combining two distinct modalities of experience ("ideas and sensations") that this extraordinarily complex definition describes, derives immediately from its origin in two separate but inextricable sources: "man" and "the objects that surround him," or "man in his own nature" (itself described as an epistemologically unravellable mix of "intuitions, and deductions, which from habit acquire the quality of intuitions"), and "in his ordinary life" (which is to say, the complex experience of "complex scene[s]" that at once enables and constitutes "ordinary life"). "Acting and re-acting upon each other," these internal and external seats of experience alternate as subject and object of the activity the poet considers, just as the actions of man, while pertaining to a single overarching process, themselves appear alternately subjective ("contemplates") and objective ("looks") in verbal mode and kind. As if

---

1. Owen and Smyser, I: 140.

this definition of the changing object that "the Poet" "considers" were not already sufficiently difficult to parse, Wordsworth repeats its terms later in the "Preface" when describing another action and its effects. The notion of "an infinite complexity of pain and pleasure" and "over-balance of enjoyment" "produce[d]" by our "interact[ion]" with the world finds its echo in the poet's description of "an over-balance of pleasure" and "complex feeling" occasioned not by the "nature" of man in view of the "objects" that "surround" him but by the effect upon a "Reader's mind" of poetry itself.[2] The natural complexity of empirical experience the poet "considers" is re-enacted, Wordsworth suggests, in the poet's representation and our consequent reception of that experience. In reading poetry we encounter the verbal "construction" of encounters with the world and thus experience a "complex feeling of delight" analogous to that experienced in living.[3] Turning the "painful feeling" that accompanies the reading of "powerful description" into one of mitigated delight, the "construction" of the poem in fact not only re-enacts experience: it allows us to surpass it and continue reading. Poetry thus *represents* experience in both senses of the word: it makes it appear present by objectifying or describing it, on the one hand, and it stands in for experience, substituting for its immediacy that of its own continuous— ideational *and* sensory—medium, on the other. For, as Wordsworth states in his contemporaneous "Note to 'The Thorn,'" the "interest" of "the mind attaches to words, not only as symbols of the passions, but as *things*, active and efficient, which are themselves part of the passion."[4]

Just as poetry and the nonverbal subjects of poetry share a common descriptive language in the "Preface," empirical experience and the experience of reading poetry so closely resemble each other in Wordsworth's poetic theory that they prove, if not theoretically identical, at least highly difficult to keep conceptually apart, and any attempt to describe Wordsworth's theory of poetry will fail to describe its own object if it "considers" what the "Poet" "does" in independence from

2. Owen and Smyser, I: 151.

3. Ibid.

4. See William Wordsworth, *Lyrical Ballads and Other Poems, 1797–1800*, ed. James Butler and Karen Green (Ithaca: Cornell University Press, 1992), p. 351. In defending "The Thorn" from the criticism that its language is repetitive, Wordsworth includes the status and effect of words used and viewed not as replaceable names for, but rather *as* "*things*" themselves "among the various other reasons why repetition and apparent tautology are frequently beauties of the highest kind" (emphasis [on "*things*"] in text).

those actions, events and objects his poetry recounts. For the interactions of man with the world and with language—the immediate effectivity of "intuitions" as distinguished from the sequential force of "deductions," no less than the unconscious transformation of the latter into the former by "habit"; the distinctive, but unpredictably interchangeable qualities and effectivities of "ideas and sensations," of verbal "expressions" and empirical encounters—are all presented by Wordsworth not only as analogous to each other but as interactive themselves: perhaps more explicitly than for any other English-language poet in history, for Wordsworth theory of poetry equals philosophy of mind.[5]

5. The interaction of language and mind noted at the opening of the "Preface" necessarily extends the confluence of philosophy of mind with poetry in Wordsworth's poetic theory to literary and social theory as well. Describing his decision not to proffer a "systematic defence of the theory upon which the [Lyrical Ballads] were written," Wordsworth notes that any such defense would have first to be prefaced by "a full account of the present state of the public taste," and that such an account could not be given in turn, "without pointing out in what manner language and the human mind act and re-act on each other, and without retracing the revolutions, not of literature alone, but likewise of society itself" (Owen and Smyser, I: 121). Recalling Rousseau's analysis, in the *Lettre á d'Alembert* (1758), of the spiraling social inequity that would be visited upon the Republic of Geneva by the introduction of commercial theatrical spectacles for whose price of admission those without means most in need of diversion would ultimately bankrupt if not sell themselves, Wordsworth describes poets who "indulge in arbitrary and capricious habits of expression" as producing and enforcing the public expectation for such expression, "furnish[ing] food for fickle tastes, and fickle appetites, of their own creation." Further echoing Rousseau's critique of the entertainments that expand in tandem with the migration of a new laboring class to urban-industrial centers, Wordsworth attributes the popularity of "frantic novels, sickly and stupid German tragedies, and deluges of idle and extravagant stories in verse" to "the increasing accumulation of men in cities, where the uniformity of their occupations produce a craving for extraordinary incident." (Owen and Smyser, I: 125, 129).

The best analytic treatment of the complex cognitive effects of Wordsworth's verbal renderings of experience remains C. C. Clarke's *Romantic Paradox. An Essay on the Poetry of Wordsworth* (London: Routledge & Kegan Paul, 1962), in which the combination of transparency and opacity created on both the lexical and syntactic levels of the poems is examined for its exact representation of the "paradox" of "sense perception" itself. In Wordsworth, Clark argues, "[t]he visionary power ... comes into being through the refinement of a more familiar

Still, in its attempt to represent the complexity of experience, to render its "infinite" nature legible, poetry, Wordsworth states, invests "powerful description" with a powerful, additional distinction. Not unlike Kant's proto-Hegelian observation in the *Critique of Judgment* of the unlimited effect upon the mind of its own ability to recognize its *inability* to form a cognition of the infinite—the recognition of the sensory limits of representation resulting in our supersensory capacity instead "*to think*" such things as number, dimension, and power beyond measure—Wordsworth adduces to poetry the singular, verbally produced power to record, name, and so proceed beyond the point at which cognitive consciousness falters. This is the power whose processes and products Wordsworth—like Kant before him—calls "sublime":[6] the

and pedestrian power, a power manifest in everyday acts of sense-perception." Yet what emerges with the poems as perception is hardly pedestrian in the commonplace sense: "distinctions between thought and the objects of thought, things and the feelings that things evoke are (at one level) suspended," Clarke observes, and "it becomes difficult for the reader to sustain without radical qualification a normal, common-sense distinction between the living and the lifeless" (pp. 41, 48–49).

6. See Kant, "Analytic of the Sublime," *Critique of Judgment* (*Kritik der Urteilskraft*; hereafter *KU*), B 92, B 110, B 115, B 116, X: 177, 189, 193, 194: "*To be able merely to think* the *given* infinite without contradiction requires a capacity in the human mind which is in itself supersensory" [Das *gegebene* Unendliche aber dennoch ohne Widerspruch *auch nur denken zu können*, dazu wird ein Vermögen, das selbst übersinnlich ist, im menschlichen Gemüte erofordert. (B 92)] "Sublimity is not contained in any thing of nature but—insofar as we can become conscious that we surpass the nature that is in us and also thereby (insofar as it influences us) the nature outside us—only in our mind" [Aber ist die Erhabenheit in keinem Dingen der Natur, sondern nur in unserem Gemüte enthalten, sofern wir der Natur in uns, und dadurch auch der Natur (sofern sie auf uns einfliesst) ausser uns, überlegen zu sein uns bewusst werden können. (B 110)]; "One can describe the sublime thus: it is an object (of nature), *whose presentation determines the mind to think to itself the unattainability of nature as a representation of ideas*" [Man kann das Erhabene so beschreiben: es ist ein Gegenstand (der Natur), *dessen Vorstellung das Gemüt bestimmt, sich die Unerreichbarkeit der Natur als Darstellung von Ideen zu denken* (B 115)]; "Literally taken and logically considered, ideas cannot be represented. But, when we widen (mathematically or dynamically) our empirical capacity for representation for the purpose of the intuition of nature, reason, as the faculty of the independence [from representation] of absolute totality, unavoidably

power to exceed representationally delimited experience in the regular employment of language that, rather than being limited, *a priori*, to sensory experience, *a posteriori*, originates and is articulated or "construct[ed]" in the active and reactive mind. While the true subject of the sublime in Kant is the subject that "judges" "sublime" its own failure to know, through objective representation, the experience of the unlimited that reason prompts it to imagine,[7] Wordsworth's poetry of

intervenes, bringing to the fore the futile striving of the mind to make sensory representation commensurate with these [ideas]. This striving, and the feeling of the unattainability of the idea through imagination, is itself a representation of the subjective purposiveness of our mind in using the imagination to determine itself in a supersensible way, and compels us subjectively *to think* nature itself in its totality as the representation of something supersensory, without being able to bring this representation into being *objectively*" [Buchstäblich genommen, und logisch betrachtet, können Ideen nicht dargestellt warden. Aber, wenn wir unser empirisches Vorstellungsvermögen (mathematisch, oder dynamisch) für die Anschauung der Natur erweitern: so tritt unausbleiblich die Vernunft hinzu, als Vermögen der Independenz der absoluten Totalität, und bringt die, obzwar vergebliche, Bestrebung des Gemüts hervor, die Vorstellung der Sinne diesen angemessen zu machen. Diese Bestrebung, und das Gefühl der Unerreichbarket der Idee durch die Einbildungskraft, ist selbst eine Darstellung der subjektiven Zweckmässigkeit unseres Gemüts in Gebrauche der Einbildungskraft für dessen übersinnliche Bestimmung, und nötigt uns, subjektiv die Natur selbst in ihrer Totalität, als Darstellung von etwas Übersinnlichem, zu *denken*, ohne diese Darstellung *objektiv* zu Stande bringen zu können. (B 116)] (emphasis in original; all translations are my own).

7. Kant, *KU* B 95, X: 179: "One thus also sees from this that true sublimity must be sought in the mind of the one who judges, not in the natural object whose judgment this determination occasions. Who would want to name unformed masses of mountains, towering above each other in wild disorder, with their pyramids of ice or gloomy roaring sea, etc. sublime? Yet the mind feels itself raised in its own judgment when, in considering these without consideration of their form, and giving itself over to imagination widened by reason set in relation to it without specific purpose, it finds the entire power of imagination incommensurate to its ideas" [Man sieht hieraus auch, dass die wahre Erhabenheit nur im Gemüte des Urteilenden, nicht in dem Naturobjekte, dessen Beurteilung diese Stimmung desselben veranlasst, müsse gesucht warden. Wer wollte auch ungestalte Gebirgmassen, in wilder Unordnung über einander getürmt, mit ihren Eispyramiden, oder die düstere tobende See, u.s.w. erhaben

the sublime uses representational language to make something infinite its very subject—a kind of action whose "construction" exchanges the identities of subject and object, like those of lived and represented experience, and the production and reception of poetics, in the course of its own ongoing progression. Whereas in Kant the sublime is another name—considered from the vantage of aesthetic judgment—for the "spontaneous act" of thinking without representation that must "accompany" all *a priori* syntheses of purely formal intuitions with empirical perception,[8] in Wordsworth it names the continuous critical

nennen? Aber das Gemüt fühlt sich in seiner eigenen Beurteilung gehoben, wenn, *indem* es sich in der Betrachtung derselben, ohne Rücksicht auf ihre Form, der Einbildungskraft, und einer, obschon ganz ohne bestimmten Zweck damit in Verbindung gesetzen, jene bloss erweiternden Vernunft, überlässt, die ganze Macht der Einbildungskraft dennoch ihren Ideen *unangemessen findet.*]

8. See Kant, "On the Synthetic Origin of the Unity of Apperception," *KrV* B 132, §16, III: 136: "The: *I think*, must *be able* to accompany all my representations; if not there would be something represented in me which could not be thought, which is as much as to say that the representation would either be impossible or at least nothing for me. The representation, which can be given before all thinking, is called *intuition* [or, purely formal perception]. Thus the entire manifold of intuitions has a necessary relation to the *I think* in the same subject in which the manifold is encountered. This representation however is an *act of spontaneity,* i.e., it cannot be viewed to belong to sensuousness. I call it *pure apperception ...*" (emphasis in text) [Das: *Ich denke,* muss alle meine Vorstellungen begleiten *können*; denn sonst würde etwas in mir vorgestellt werden was gar nicht gedacht werden könnte, welches eben so viel heisst, als die Vorstellung würde entweder unmöglich, oder wenigstens für mich nichts sein. Diejenige Vorstellung, die vor allem Denken gegeben sein kann, heisst *Anschauung.* Also hat alles Mannigfaltige der Anschauung eine notwendige Beziehung auf das: *Ich denke,* in demselben Subjekt, darin diese Mannigfaltige angetroffen wird. Diese Vorstellung aber ist ein Actus der *Spontaneität,* d.i., sie kann nicht als zur Sinnlichkeit gehörig angesehen werden. Ich nenne sie die reine *Apperzeption . . . .*]

In the unfinished manuscript posthumously entitled "The Sublime and the Beautiful," published as Appendix III to the *Guide through the District of the Lakes* (MSS. Prose 28) in Owen and Smyser (II: 349–360), and probably written around 1811, Wordsworth, discussing the sublime in relation not to poetry but to the "visible object[s]" presented by "forms of Nature," partially incorporates Kant's thesis regarding the real location of the sublime in describing it as an experience of "intense unity" between the "mind" of the "Spectator" and an difficulty of distinguishing thinking from representation in the first place, a difficulty both historical and immediate—or, in Wordsworth's terms—"poetic" in quality. In Wordsworth's practice of "what the Poet [does]," representation itself becomes a medium of thought.

What is *not* difficult to distinguish, however, is the marked contrast drawn in Wordsworth's poetic theory between the nature of the subject of poetry and its means. Accompanying the affirmation of the "infinite complexity" of experience the poet "considers" is the very different argument Wordsworth makes regarding the noncomplex nature of the language of the poet's "powerful descriptions," the single thesis, regarding poetic language, for which the "Preface" is best known. That thesis is memorable not only for its own directness of exposition but because, appearing in a "Preface" to poems its author has already written, it articulates and re-represents critically the acts of representation committed in them. Giving a second intellectual life to the "complex feeling" effected by the poems' particular verbal "construction," Wordsworth's explicit exposition of a poetics arising from and productive of experience itself recasts an apparently idiosyncratic style of authorship into a watershed event in poetic history.[9] For, in making

---

"external power": "To talk of an object as being sublime or beautiful in itself, without references to some subject by whom that sublimity or beauty is perceived, is absurd" (see II: 350–357 [357]). Despite frequent disclaimers that he had ever read it, Wordsworth's familiarity with the interrelated premises and overarching structure of Kant's *Critique* is most clearly indicated in this later work by his own repeated relation of the sublime to "the moral law": "it may be confidently said that, unless the apprehensions which [the Power contemplated] excites terminate in repose, there can be no sublimity, & that this sense of repose is the result of reason and the moral law" (II: 355; see also 356, 357). On Wordsworth's avowed ignorance of Kant's writings, see Duncan Wu, *Wordsworth's Reading 1800-1815* (Cambridge: Cambridge University Press, 1998), pp. 261–262.

9. In *Wordsworth's Theory of Poetic Diction* (New Haven: Yale University Press, 1917), Marjorie Latta Barstow argued early for the consonance of Wordsworth's view of poetic language with that which characterized English poetry before the seventeenth century. While Barstow also astutely remarks on Wordsworth's endeavor "to make his syntax reflect the movements of impassioned thought," her equation of Wordsworth's "interest in words" with an interest in "metaphors" capable of "substitut[ing] imagery for language," seems particularly misplaced (pp. 126, 177). For a contrasting view of Wordsworth's "simplicity" of style as a devaluation of the verbal in itself, see John Danby, *The*

an analysis of the qualities of poetic language the central thrust and substance of a "Preface" to his own poems, Wordsworth, writing as critic, not only calls attention to the specificity of the historical moment in which, as poet, he himself has written, but suggests that the break with the contemporary poetic landscape the *Lyrical Ballads* enact stems less from any passing personal predilection than a general truth about poetry, a permanent theoretical necessity concerning language generally and so extending beyond individual authors and poems.

Defying the critically enshrined styles of Donne, Dryden, and Pope, the theory of poetic language contained within the larger theory of poetry presented in the "Preface" proceeds, like Wordsworth's analysis of the subject of poetry, along both internal (or actively effective) and external (in this case, arbitrarily established) lines. That internal theory, defining both the language constitutive of poems and the contours of the history of their reception, lays the groundwork for the scathing narration of fads and frauds exposed, in the later "Essay, Supplementary to the Preface" (1815), to constitute popular "taste," even as it takes the ground out from under all familiar and accepted doctrine of poetic form. Famously "reject[ing]" the special "use," or abuse, of language conventionally assumed to identify the presence of poetry—the pointedly artificial stylization of language he calls "poetic diction"—in favor of the language he variously, and always necessarily inadequately, describes as "the language really used by men . . .," "the very language of men . . .," or, simply, "the language of men," Wordsworth defines poetic language in the "Preface" as ultimately having *no* defining characteristics, nothing that would distinguish its individual words as inherently different from those composing the language employed by all:

> If in a poem there should be found a series of lines, or even a single
> line, in which the language, though naturally arranged, and according

Simple Wordsworth (London: Routledge & Kegan Paul, 1971 [1960]), p. 16: "Wordsworth, at heart, we might say, was profoundly uninterested in poetry as words." Observing, nonetheless, that Wordsworth was "committed . . . to the public necessity of utterance," the nonverbal proclivity Danby attributes to this inordinately voluminous poet underscores, however perversely, the same "public" nature of the language to whose "utterance" Wordsworth similarly "committed" both his theory of poetry composed of "the language really used by men," and the proximity of the experience of language to the experience of experience in his poems.

to the strict laws of metre, does not differ from that of prose, there is a numerous class of critics, who, when they stumble upon these prosaisms, as they call them, imagine that they have made a notable discovery, and exult over the Poet as over a man ignorant of his own profession. Now these men would establish a canon of criticism which the Reader will conclude he must utterly reject, if he wishes to be pleased with these volumes. And it would be a most easy task to prove to him, that not only the language of a large portion of every good poem, even of the most elevated character, must necessarily, except with reference to the metre, in no respect differ from that of good prose, but likewise that some of the most interesting parts of the best poems will be found to be strictly the language of prose when prose is well written.[10]

Attacking those "critics" who, in canonizing what counts as poetry, effectively enforce a larger misunderstanding of the active basis of our relation to language in general, Wordsworth memorably dubs all such "pre-established codes of decision" "the most dreadful enemy of our pleasures": by cordoning off the "poetic" from the "prosaic," he argues, such self-appointed arbiters threaten to render not only language as such but with it our own "real" capacity for experience inert. Disentangling the act of poetry-writing from all the accoutrements of a specialized "profession"—exclusionary status, rules of procedure, an added professional "class" societally authorized to monitor and oversee these, and, for its practitioners, privileged access to specialized tools[11]— Wordsworth proceeds to prove his point by way of direct textual interpretation. Citing, *verbatim*, a sonnet by Gray, he highlights the sole lines in it he deems "of any value" so as to demonstrate that, just as the diction of those lines do not, "the language of every good poem can in no respect differ from that of good Prose."[12] From this observation of the interchangeable quality of poetry and prose, Wordsworth proceeds to formulate a premise of non-distinction between the two genres, equating them not only as they appear in individual instances of traditional forms (as words assembled into the traditional textual shape of a sonnet, for example), but as what, in all instances, in "essence[e]," they are (i.e., words, available for assemblage into any text and in any

10. Owen and Smyser, I: 131, 161, 137, 142, 123, 131, 133.
11. See "Advertisement," in Owen and Smyser, I: 116–117 (116).
12. Owen and Smyser, I: 135.

context whatsoever): "We will go further. It may be safely affirmed that
there neither is, nor can be, any *essential* difference between the language
of prose and metrical composition"; "they require and exact one and the
same language."[13]

Even the single distinguishing feature Wordsworth grants poetry
initially—that of its accommodation and conveyance of "meter," the
combination of number, stress pattern and natural inflection that carries
linear verbal sequences forward—is quickly undermined in the "Preface"
as Wordsworth "go[es] further" still, redefining the absence of any
"*essential* difference" between poetry and prose to encompass the given,
extra-lexical rhythms he had ascribed to the "metrical composition"
of poetry alone. In a footnote to the word "'Poetry'"—one of only
two notes, and the only extended one, appearing in the "Preface"—
Wordsworth criticizes the fallacy of understanding the word (itself
placed between quotation marks by Wordsworth) as "synonymous with
metrical composition," noting that "passages of meter" not only routinely
"occur" in prose as well but do so "so naturally" "that it would be scarcely
possible to avoid them."[14] Thus, any theoretical attempt to distinguish
the language *and* composition of "Poetry" from those of "Prose," as if
these were different rather than two of a kind (as, Wordsworth admits,
"against [his] own judgment," he himself had just cursorily done), will
contribute no helpful knowledge to the "criticism" of poetry but, rather,
cause further "confusion" as to its real nature and effects. True knowledge
of what constitutes poetry depends instead, Wordsworth suggests, on
our ability to identify that to which "Poetry" is neither lexically, nor
metrically, but rather "philosophical[ly]" opposed—not so-called "Prose"
writing but any writing whose sole aim is to establish "Matter[s] of Fact":

> (1) I here use the word "Poetry" (though against my own judgment)
> as opposed to the word Prose, and synonymous with metrical
> composition. But much confusion has been introduced into criticism
> by this contradistinction of Poetry and Prose, instead of the more
> philosophical one of Poetry and Matter of Fact, or Science. The only
> strict antithesis to Prose is Metre; nor is this, in truth, a *strict* antithesis,
> because lines and passages of metre so naturally occur in writing prose,
> that it would be scarcely possible to avoid them, even were it desirable.[15]

13. Ibid. (emphasis in text); "Appendix" to the "Preface," I: 164.
14. Owen and Smyser, I: 135.
15. Ibid. (emphasis in text).

Reviewing and revising his own previous statement, Wordsworth replaces the sensuous and numerical aspect of poetry he now no longer considers "strict[ly]" opposed to that of prose with an opposition between poetry and that discourse concerned solely with denoting the givens of purely external sensuous "matter," i.e., "fact[s]" whose existence is independent of language itself. Unlike the discourse of "Poetry" *and* "Prose," the verbal recording of physical reality by "Science" (epitomized ideally not in discourse but number alone) must, by definition, take no account of the subject's experience of its objects, and the different bases of the involvements of "Science" and poetics with matter—the externality of the material world required for the annotation of "Matter[s] of Fact" by the former, and the inextricability of that world to the complex experience of it that "Poetry" in particular attempts to represent—indeed prove central to Wordsworth's own poetic subject matter and practice. Just as the verbal line of cadence and meter supposed to separate poetry from prose serves no less, Wordsworth observes, to link them, the properly "philosophical" distinction to which Wordsworth's consideration of the problem progresses results in a poetics dependent upon the very "prosaisms" conventionally condemned by poetasters. For the difference between poetry and prose at which Wordsworth's note ultimately arrives focuses not on any internal distinction, let alone "pre-established codes," but on the different relationships different kinds of writing bear to common external objects. In contrast to both the classification of empirical matter as unrelated and thus recordable "Matter[s] of Fact," and the evasion and replacement of empirical experience by purely ornamental figures and stock topoi deemed "poetic," "Poetry," Wordsworth argues, strives to represent the inherently differential, temporal and eventful nature of our interaction with the material world, or, as he states of the engagement with the empirical involved in producing "poems so materially different" as his own from the "poetic" norm: "I have at all times endeavoured to look steadily at my subject." Based not on "pre-established codes" or norms for manipulating pointedly artificial terms, but unanticipated experiences of a noncodified external world, "Poetry," as Wordsworth defines it, must exclude as extraneous all those verbal devices whose only semantic function is to connote the presence of "poetic diction" among them.[16]

16. In more contemporary critical parlance, such devices pertain to the set of "second-order" signs, or "meta-language," that Barthes identified as the signifiers of the over-saturated, "motivated" signifieds conveyed by modern social "myths."

Wordsworth's critical aversion to the "mechanical" use of "figure[s] of speech" in poetry is well known.[17] Taking direct aim at the detachable "ornaments" that "from father to son have long been regarded as the common inheritance of Poets," Wordsworth theorizes for the first time in literary history a poetics and poetry of commonplace language—the so-called "ordinary" language common to all—whose principles and practice, while "so materially different from those upon which general approbation is at present bestowed," became (and have remained) the origin from which the practice of most modern poetry, as well as most modern English-language philosophy, descends.[18] Like Kant's interrelated theories of inherently "discursive" cognition and a universal faculty of judgment "grounded" in a linguistic "common sense," Wordsworth's poetic theory effects a "revolution" in our understanding of its object, effectively inventing the "real"—i.e., practically productive— "language" of poetry it describes.[19] Indeed, "the revolution in mode of thinking" to which Kant repeatedly ascribes the origination of the fundamental "constructive" principles of geometry, the analogous, scientifically groundbreaking "hypotheses" of Galilean and Copernican astronomy, and, by direct implication, his own equally upending,

---

Like the "naturalness" of French colonialism, or the "bountiful" "nature" of plastic, whose always semi-tautological "mythologies" of signification Barthes analyzes, the "imperative" signified, "Poetry," imposed upon the reader by the presence of otherwise senseless "poetic" ornaments resembles nothing so much as the necessarily overdetermined content of advertisements for commercial products: "This is poetry, because poetry is this." See Roland Barthes, *Mythologies* (Paris: Les lettres nouvelles, 1957), esp. pp. 193–243 (Eng. trans. Anette Lavers [New York: Farrar Strauss and Giroux, 1972], esp. pp. 109–153).

17. Owen and Smyser, I: 131.

18. Owen and Smyser, I: 133.

19. For Kant's definition of all cognition as "discursive," see Kant, *Logik* A 221–222, VI: 576; *KrV* B XXIV, III: 29; for Kant's hypothesis of a "power to judge" ("Urteilskraft") predicated on the specifically verbal capacity for "general communicability" that he enigmatically dubs "common sense," see Kant, *KU* B 65, §20, X: 157. I treat the centrality of our capacity to act in language to Kant's theory of judgment in the Third Critique and, in its explicit relation to judgment, to the very "possibility" of moral action hypothesized in the Second Critique, in Claudia Brodsky, *The Linguistic Condition. Kant's Critique of Judgment and the Poetics of Action* (London: Bloomsbury (forthcoming, 2020)), the companion volume to the present work.

"hypothetical" *Critique* of our fundamental capacities—for cognition, aesthetic experience, moral action, and political formation—is precisely indicative of the internal, "no less than" social, "revolutions" Wordsworth ascribes to the interactions of "language and the human mind . . ., of literature . . . [and] of society itself."[20] Yet the "materially different" language Wordsworth seeks to define is not merely the result of a poetics aimed at deflating the vanity of figurative displays or confined in content to the goal of stylistic change.[21] While the apparent simplicity of Wordsworth's poetic language is frequently belittled for resembling that of its least artful speakers—the "simple Child" reiterating a single arithmetic sum to an interlocutor "throwing words away" in the attempt to induce her to distinguish the living from the dead, in "We are Seven";[22] the eponymous "Idiot Boy," who, asked to report "true" what he "ha[d] seen" "all this long night," responds by mimicking a rooster crowing: "that was all his travel's story"[23]—in a more significant sense, the prosaic diction Wordsworth advocates and employs poses a conceptual challenge to the very thesis of poetically rendered "complexity" the "Preface" presents.

20. See n.5, this Chapter (Owen and Smyser, I: 121). For "revolution in mode of thinking" ("Revolution der Denkart"), see Kant *KrV* B vii, xi, xiv, xv, xvi, xxii, xxx, III: 20, 22– 25, 28, 33.

21. Owen and Smyser, I: 121.

22. Owen and Smyser, ll. 1, 65–69.

23. Owen and Smyser, ll. 439–41, 453.

Chapter 3

"What the Poet Does"

Having described the "complex" subject matter "the poet ... considers" as a "*scene* of ideas and sensations"—a partly intellectual, partly sensory object of vision (as well as hearing and other modes of perception) composed as much of the poet's "contemplati[on]" of the external world as of the internal "habit[s]" formed in the course of such contemplation—Wordsworth's theory of poetry must still define the language that can convey the combined ordinariness and extraordinariness of the experience the poet would relate. In order to render in any commensurate measure an already "complex scene," poetic language, Wordsworth suggests, cannot resort to extraneous, artificial means. Rather than serving up markers of the "poetic" without referent, the language capable of describing such a "scene" must be representational, and therein available to our own internal "visualization" of its objects and aspects in coordination with its narrative—temporal and sequential—development. Just as the complexity upon which the poet "looks" is itself both product and component of dynamic interactions with a world with a life of its own, for Wordsworth the language of poetry must follow the progress of the actual as well as repetitively internalized "experience" of reality it names. Only "a language arising out of repeated experience and regular feelings," he cautions, can constitute the "more permanent" and "far more philosophical language" of poetry, i.e., a language that, in the very act of representing the complexity of experience, itself "communicates with the best objects from which the best part of language is originally derived."[1] The conventions of "poetic diction" impede precisely the "communicat[ion]" of subject–object, language–object, and subject–language relations, Wordsworth esteems, and it is his intention to further that hybrid linguistic history by participating in and actualizing it, "avoid[ing]" reified linguistic terms and codes so as to come closer to language as it "derive[s]" from living

---

1. Owen and Smyser, I: 125.

in and interacting with the world and with language itself, the representation and qualification of real experience that constitutes "the real language of men."[2] Here, the future of "real language" (or "permanence," for Wordsworth, of poetry itself) depends on its beginning—its being instantiated—in "communicat[ion]" with the experience it articulates, again and again. Only if composed in "the language really used by men" will "poetry" transmit the kind of "powerful description" capable of rendering "scenes" of experience objects of experience themselves; only in representing rather than replacing those "objects" of experience from which "the best part of language is originally derived" does the writing of poetry give rise to a common language in which the very ability of language to convey the content of experience is communicated as well.

In view of Wordsworth's definition of "what ... the Poet [does]," his transformative proposition that the languages of poetry and prose are not two but one inevitably raises the following, critical question: how can words presented and read as noncomplex—as intentionally lacking in the gratuitous logical complications, lexical-semantic "abuses," and inter- and intralinguistic conceits Wordsworth condemns[3]—represent, on the one hand, the complex *empirical* experience every subject undergoes, and, on the other, take part in the *verbal* "construction" of that experience such as every poet worth reading composes? For the unifying insight tying the world to man and man to words in the "Preface" is that both the experience of everyday, circumstantial "objects" and the "description," in poetry, of the "feelings," "ideas" and "sensations" such experience entails, involve not simplicity or simplicity only, but rather the kind of complexity that poetry alone can represent. For, even when employing the simplest of referential terms, the "purpose" toward which, according to Wordsworth, all poetry "worthy of the name" aims, is the communication of "scenes" of experience as "complex" as it

2. Owen and Smyser, I: 131.

3. First among these "abuses" in the "Preface" is "the personification of abstract ideas" (Owen and Smyser, I: 161, 131). In the "Appendix" to the "Preface," Wordsworth further adumbrates and excoriates the forms of "what is usually called Poetic Diction": "invented" "modes of expression," "unusual language" and "adulterated phraseology"—a "motley masquerade of tricks, quaintnesses, hieroglyphics, and enigmas" that, "imported from one nation to another" without experiential substantiation or reproof "became daily more and more corrupt" (Owen and Smyser, I: 161–162).

renders the identity of those simple referents themselves. This appears the purpose of the dynamic actions serially staged and represented in *The Prelude*, actions aimed precisely at exceeding the limits of representational cognition itself: "the visible scene" that "would enter unawares into [the] mind" of the silenced Boy of Winander, "[w]ith all its solemn imagery, its rocks,/Its woods, and the uncertain heaven, received/Into the bosom of the steady lake"; the scene of a "sky that seemed not a sky/Of earth," the "motion [that] moved the clouds" unknown, to the boy "hang[ing] above a raven's nest" "suspended" or "(so it seemed)" . . . by the blast that blew amain."[4]

And yet how, in the absence of recognizable representational language, can the relation of sky to earth be reported to change? How can simplicity yield complexity, the representation of familiar referents yield unrecognizable scenes, and the ordinary language of their designation and description "communicate" a sense of the extraordinary? What, in short, in Wordsworth's theory of poetry, *does* distinguish prosaic simplicity ("'Seven are we'") from sublime complexity ("Nay, we are seven"), prose from poetry, the experience of the "real language" that the "Preface" first defines from non-poetic conceptions either of reality or of language overall?

For true complexity, Wordsworth contends, derives not from the selective presence of rarified verbal figures but the omnipresence of the prosaic, now understood to include not only the objects and language of lived experience, but the content of the poetic itself. In declining at the opening of the "Preface" to write "a systematic defense of the theory upon which the[se] Poems were written," Wordsworth begs the question of whether the "real language" and reality of experience whose complex interaction all poetry worthy of the name represents, is any more amenable to defense or systematization than human life itself.[5] Necessarily treated as equivalent, if not identical, both by categorical "systems-philosophies" (from Aristotle through Luhmann), and non-philosophical approaches to "culture" equating all cultural production with the prescriptions of an exhaustive autotelic system (whether generated, on the model of biology, by a supposedly autonomous power of "autopoiesis," or statically reflective of an all-pervasive social "power" of total domination), the semantic and technical components of language,

---

4. Wordsworth, *The Fourteen-Book Prelude*, ed. W. J. B. Owen (Ithaca: Cornell University Press, 1985), V: 384–388, p. 193; I: 330–339, p. 55 (hereafter *The Prelude*, followed by Book and line numbers).

5. Owen and Smyser, I: 121.

by direct contrast, are never conflated or equated by Wordsworth. Made "real" *by* its active relation to experience, the "language really used by men," of which both poetry and prose are composed, instead excludes, on Wordsworth's definition, all predetermined (esoteric or *sui generis,* socially prescribed, or "poetic") codes of diction and content, just as the theory of such a language must break with the purely nominal notions of the verbal required for the subordination of all utterance to a "meaning"-system.

If Wordsworth's own poetic diction, like that of the works of Chaucer and Milton he commends, is marked by its prosaic nature—the immediate accessibility of its literal sense—and if both poetic rhetoric and theoretical systematicity are set aside in the "Preface," and the prosaic, posited in their place, then the question regarding Wordsworth's definition of poetry, now reflectively "redoubled" (in the words of his poetry[6]) by its own purposeful theoretical description, remains: what is the source of the complexity of the reading experience, like that of dynamic empirical experience, that poetry both sets into motion and represents? Indeed, it can be argued more generally that the relationship of Wordsworth's theory of poetics to his poetry—the addition of conscious reflection by the former to the prosaic representation of experiences recounted by the latter—is the poet-theorist's attempt to "answer" in *critical* terms the misplaced insistence of the Boy of Winander that his own "mimic hootings" be imitated or "echoed" *as if they were or could ever be made the same* as the nature they unnaturally provoke. For, in using *sensory imitation* to compel "silent owls" to mimic his learned ability to mimic them. the Boy inadvertently engenders no pleasing concert of animal nature and human techne but a "din" of indistinguishable sound emptied of any perceptible sense, just as Wordsworth's *verbal representation* of the Boy proves, by direct contrast, that the very notion of "nature poetry" (*pace* the poet's own critics) is a contradiction in terms.[7]

Unlike the willful imposition of senseless figures, on the one hand, or of mimicry emptied of sense, on the other, "complex feeling" in

---

6. *The Prelude,* V: 378.

7. See Ibid., V: 373–385. The drowning of the Boy's sensory imitation in a flood of non-sense ceasing as abruptly as it started—"echoes loud /Redoubled and redoubled; concourse wild/Of jocund din" issuing from creatures he pointedly does *not* resemble—leaves the Boy, in Wordsworth's remarkable, reiterative phrase, "sometimes" "h[a]ng[ing]" in a death-like state of suspension.

Wordsworth's view is neither systematically induced nor synchronic in effect but the process of losing one's sense of balance in perceiving, whether through words or in the world, the "complex scene" of experience itself. Just as experience simplified of its complexity would be experience missed, poetry amenable to systematic theoretical defense would not be poetry in any real, practical sense, and certainly not the necessary mode of representing and extending experience Wordsworth suggests. For "[t]he end of Poetry," he states, is not merely to memorialize and report experience past, but to effect the actual dynamism of "complex" experience in the mind of its present reader: "to produce excitement in co-existence with an over-balance of pleasure."[8]

Yet in the course of actively producing such excitement without the hindrance of stilted "poetic diction," poetry, like experience, may well put complexity of experience at risk. Wordsworth recognizes that the composition of complexity may also occasion its demise, that "[i]f the words ... by which this excitement is produced be in themselves powerful, or the images and feelings have an undue proportion of pain connected with them, there is some danger that the excitement may be carried beyond its proper bounds."[9] In order for "Poetry" to achieve its "end," i.e., the creation of a "complex scene" of experience capable of "produc[ing]" the "co-existence" of powerful feelings within the reader, it must add to its use of "real language" something simple rather than complex. Rather than submit to its own preclusion by either abstractly systematizing description or artificially complicated "poetic diction," the experience of reading must include something capable of actively counteracting the "over-balance" of feeling it brings about. As perceptible as are physical objects to our senses, that something is no substantial thing but the "co-presence of something regular," the "laws" and "charm" exercised upon our minds by the "greatly underrated ... power of metre."[10]

Radically severed from all possibility of response, the Boy's virtuosic technique yields nothing less than an absolute end to sensation, a "mute[ness]" of the kind the poet soon after similarly refers reiteratively to himself, as his narrative turns from the Boy stilled by "a gentle shock of mild surprise," to "[t]his" same "Boy" soon "taken from his mates," and the "summer evenings ... I have stood/Mute, looking at the grave in which [the Boy] lies" (V: 395–97).

8. Owen and Smyser, I: 147.
9. Ibid.
10. Ibid.

It is meter that, already alternately described by Wordsworth as distinguishing and uniting poetry and prose,[11] carries us past such abrupt "fits" of "feeling," just as "hoof after hoof" climbing on horseback toward Lucy's cottage, or like water "struck and struck again" in the attempt to row away from a "power" visibly "growing still,"[12] something "regular" allows the boy and Poet to proceed: to live past overpowering experience, and compose poetry of it, in the "language really used by men." Neither imagined nor conceptual, meter is specifically attributed by Wordsworth with the ability to join poetry to the actual experience of the world by extending both in time in such a way as to make them available to thought, and it is at this point that what may well be both the most familiar and most mangled quotation in the history of poetic theory in English—the apparent non sequitur beginning, "For all good poetry …"—must be afforded the full reading its own extensive definition of "poetry," as the active extension of experience into thinking, deserves.

11. See Chap. 2, n. 15.

12. *The Prelude,* I: 379–382 [I: 407–409]; for detailed analyses of the incident of the stolen boat, see Part I, Chap. 6, and Part II, Chap. 10, this study.

Chapter 4

The Poetics of Contradiction

In the case of this celebrated description, best known is also least known or, as Wordsworth might have written, most complex. While Wordsworth opens his most famous definition with the apparently simple observation: "For all good poetry is the spontaneous overflow of powerful feelings: ...," that introductory statement, as its immediate punctuation (":") indicates, is only part of a longer thought, one whose continuation after the full colon connecting it to what follows it contradicts, without effacing, the assertion with which it had begun.

The truncated version of Wordsworth's definition has long been the single lens through which his own work is most readily, while disparately, viewed: embraced for its anti-intellectualism, rejected as ideologically mystified, or dismissed as irremediably naïve. Considered in its entirety, however, Wordsworth's bifurcating definition of poetry contradicts not only itself but the larger argument regarding the motivation and agency of poetry that directly preceded it in the "Preface."[1] For, immediately previous to the opening assertion—"For

---

1. The disfiguring abbreviation of this quotation in Wordsworth criticism is nearly co-extensive with that criticism itself. Its pervasiveness is perhaps best indicated in small by a fine recent study unusually questioning its claim on Wordsworth himself. In suggesting that, though he "became famous for equating the best poetry with a spontaneous overflow of feeling," Wordsworth, some fourteen years after writing the "Preface," expressed "second thoughts about this expression," Susan Wolfson still adheres to the traditional truncated version of Wordsworth's divided definition, omitting to mention the extensive second half in which exactly such "second" (third, fourth, indeed, innumerable) "thoughts" are already both evidenced *and* declared necessary to "poetry" of "any" worth (see citation of full quotation below, in which the word "best" is not only never mentioned but, rather, "the only poetry to which any value can be attached" is directly attributed instead to the *act* of having "thought long and deeply" in a progressive series of actions undertaken in reaction to such "spontaneous"

all good poetry is the spontaneous overflow of powerful feelings ..."—
Wordsworth had asserted the opposite: that not a sudden surfeit of
"powerful feelings" but, rather, "habits of meditation" long undergone,
first endowed his *Lyrical Ballads* with the single defining attribute
of poetry.[2] That attribute regards not the origin but the *aim* of any

"feeling"). While limiting her comparison of remarks to the words preceding
Wordsworth's full colon punctuation, Wolfson cites a letter of 1814 in which the
poet briefly reprises the view *already expressed* in the extensive second part of
his sentence, which, at once divided from and equated with its initial assertion
by that full colon, directly conjoins "spontaneous overflow" to the opposing
poetic necessity of a diachronic experience of "thought." For the personalized,
incidental version of that larger theoretical view, see Wolfson, citing Wordsworth,
in "Wordsworth's Craft," *The Cambridge Companion to Wordsworth*, ed. Stephen
Gill (Cambridge: Cambridge University Press, 2003), pp. 108–124 (123): "'My
first expressions I often find detestable; and it is frequently true of second words
as of second thoughts, that they are the best.'"

By contrast, James A. W. Heffernan's canonical study of Wordsworth's poetic
theory provides a kind of baseline indication of how little the full definition is
actually *read*. For, even as he takes the highly unusual step of citing Wordsworth's
complex sentence in its entirety, Heffernan chooses to omit the explicit meaning
of its second half in his commentary, asserting that, for Wordsworth,
"consciousness plays no part in the creative act itself," in open contradiction
with the clearly stated theoretical argument it is the burden of the complete
sentence to convey. See Heffernan, *Wordsworth's Theory of Poetry* (Ithaca:
Cornell University Press, 1969), p. 43.

Why such willful blindness to the worth of the actual words Wordsworth
chose to use, not in private correspondence or otherwise obscure or passing
fashion, but in the explanatory "Preface" he expressly added to the publication
of his inaugural body of poems with the overt intention of reminding the
public, *pace* the cultural caste system enforced by paid taste-makers, not only of
the "real language" in which all true, or "permanent" poetry consists, but how
poems "of any value" come, through a process of "deep and long" "thought," to be
written—why such equally overt misrepresentation and mistaken textual
transmission persists with regard not only to Wordsworth's poetry (frequent
synecdoche for "Romantic" poetry and "Romanticism"), but to something
explicitly entitled "Wordsworth's theory of poetry," and from what motivation
the deformation of that "theory" into a kind of *anti*-theory opposing "thought"
of any kind arises, are problems of historicization whose etiology lies outside
the purview of the current study.

   2. Owen and Smyser, I: 127.

poetic work, the enigmatic, nearly eponymous object Wordsworth calls "a worthy *purpose*."[3] Rather than reflect an internal state of agitation, it is the ability of poetry to convey something outside it, that, at the same time, could not be "formally conceived" without it, which alone defines for Wordsworth what it is to be a poem, i.e., words committed to the course of a specific kind of action of their own. Suggesting that, if they themselves do not "carry along with them a *purpose*," his own poems should not be considered—and only on that condition not considered—to have been poems in the first place, he further forfeits any personal claim to the general designation, "Poet," should his understanding of what constitutes poetry be flawed: "If this opinion be erroneous, I can have little right to the name of a Poet."[4]

Following, thus, upon a categorical notion of poetic "purpose" extending to his own work, and extensive descriptions of reflective and habitual mental processes that spontaneity can neither eradicate nor contain, the full statement of the first sentence of Wordsworth's most frequently and least completely quoted definition of poetry proceeds as follows:

> For all good poetry is the spontaneous overflow of powerful feelings: and though this be true, Poems to which any value can be attached were never produced on any variety of subjects but by a man who, being possessed of more than usual organic sensibility, had also thought long and deeply.[5]

Combining spontaneity with duration, feeling with thinking, and overflow with depth, this internally divided definition of those "Poems to which any value can be attached" enacts the very notion of complexity at the core of the poet's poetic theory. Small wonder that such an apparently self-contradictory definition, so inherently difficult to summarize, has been regularly misleadingly abbreviated in the course of its repetition, and that, despite—or because of—its nearly rote transmission, it has rarely been cited, let alone analyzed, as, in fact, written, i.e., *including the connective full colon that*, following directly upon its opening assertion, immediately directs the reader to read

3. Owen and Smyser, I: 125 (emphasis in text).
4. Owen and Smyser, I: 127.
5. Ibid.

beyond the "powerful feeling" it names.[6] Indeed, likewise composed *in full* of its own explicit internal contradiction, this is a definition that begs definition by any singular compositional trait. Still further disturbing to the attribution to Wordsworth of a derisorily simplistic concept of poetry (and, through Wordsworth, to the latter-day formation of a caricature of anti-"rationalism" called "Romanticism," whose supposed rejection of all forms of "thought" and reflection, as mere impediments to the greater aim of expressing the subjectivity of emotions, he is portrayed to exemplify), the long explanatory sentence immediately following this self-contradictory one seeks nonetheless to do just that, i.e., to define what Wordsworth's paradoxical definition cannot. Composed of a series of individually complete clauses, each of which runs counter to the internally divided definition it succeeds, this extraordinarily extensive sentence delineates in specific verbal detail the "act[s]" of representation, repetition, mental habit, and abstraction that, according to Wordsworth, produce poetry by occurring not singly and spontaneously but together *and* sequentially, which is to say, differentially, and thus, necessarily, temporally: discrete, non-interchangeable acts taking place over time in the mind:

> For our continued influxes of feeling are modified and directed by our thoughts, which are indeed the representatives of all our past feelings; and, as by contemplating the relation of these general representatives to each other, we discover what is really important to men, so by the repetition and continuance of this *act*, our feelings will

6. Attempts to account for the consistent curtailment of Wordsworth's definition of poetry by its historical reception will recall that, toward the end of the "Preface," the poet apparently contributes to that distortion by quoting his own definition only in part, stopping, at first, at the full colon marking its internal division, as if reproducing in advance the future reversal of his meaning in transmission. Yet, here, too, Wordsworth proceeds immediately to *contradict* the initial, unilateral assertion he himself has just cited by reiterating, in its full extension and complexity, the "deeply" reflective acts he defined as essential to poetic composition within the single, original sentence. For the complete text of Wordsworth's quotation of himself, see Chap. 5, n. 2. See Chap. 4, n. 5 and n. 7 together, for the full text of the definition and its own immediate, extraordinarily detailed extension, in the elaboration of the several heterogenous, temporally and formally differentiated actions and practices defined to comprise "thought" in the sentence directly following it in the "Preface."

be connected with important subjects, till at length, if we be originally possessed of much sensibility, such habits of mind will be produced, that, by obeying blindly and mechanically the impulses of those habits, we shall describe objects, and utter sentiments, of such a nature, and in such connection with each other, that the understanding of the Reader must necessarily be in some degree enlightened, and his affection strengthened and purified.[7]

In this thoroughly progressive version of the representational subject of poetry—of "man" and "objects" "acting and reacting upon each other"—the "objects" poetry "describe[s]" and the "sentiments" it "utter[s]" are not only not given, but first arise in a manner as removed as any imaginable from the evanescent opposite of givens, the unprecedented and unpredicated non sequitur that "is" a "spontaneous overflow of ... feeling." Rather than springing into being within us on the model of what we call "emotions"—feelings imitative of "exiting" physical "motions" in that they exceed our ability to contain or understand them—the "objects" and "sentiments" that poetry represents are defined here as "of such a nature, and in such connection with each other, that the understanding of the Reader must necessarily be in some degree *enlightened*" by their "descri[ption]" (emphasis added). Furthermore, rather than "feeling" as such, it is the "direct[ion]" of "continuous influxes of feeling ... by our thoughts" that makes possible the making of poetry, such that acts of thinking are considered distinct from, yet not opposed to "powerful feeling" within Wordsworth's full exposition of the course of changing present-tense actions ("*are* modified and directed ... *are* representatives ... by *contemplating* we *discover* ...) that is constitutive of "Poetry." "Thoughts" are instead what Wordsworth now generally calls "the representatives of all our past feelings," and it is in "contemplating" such "representatives" in their "relation" to each other; in the "repetition and continuance of this act"; and, ultimately, in our "blind" and "mechanical" obedience to the "impulses" of "habit," or non-thought, that such repetition "produce[s]" over time—ongoing "impulses" produced and reproduced within ourselves analogous to the rhythmic beats and stresses of meter—that, Wordsworth sequentially recounts, poetry of any value first comes about.

Yet "first" is a particularly elusive concept within the context of its elaboration here. For Wordsworth's definition of poetry begins with a

---

7. Owen and Smyser, I : 127 (emphasis added).

premise whose development leads, by the very scope of that definition, to its transformation. The "repetition" of the "act" of "contemplating" "relations" between "the representatives of all our past feelings," or "thoughts," and the "mechanical" obedience to such "habits of mind" as that repetitive act entails, intervene upon and change the experience of "spontaneous feeling," the effect of the "continuance" of the former necessarily altering the "continued influx" of the latter. This is not to say that feeling and thinking, immediacy and habit, cancel each other out for Wordsworth, any more than the experience of temporal extension can exclude its interruption by spontaneous events. It does suggest, however, that in describing the composition of poetry as requiring complex, i.e., internally experienced *and* linguistically committed, or "representative," actions, rather than a merely passive submission to either the "spontaneous" advent of "powerful feeling" or the historical clout of meretriciously "complex," hypertrophied "poetic diction," Wordsworth's definition—narrative rather than apodictic in character— describes an experience unilaterally unattributable to either its truncated first, or extensive second part.

Chapter 5

"The True Difficulty"

Read in its entirety, the complexity of Wordsworth's definition of poetry matches that of its subject. As described in the "Preface" and—as described in the following analyses—instantiated in the poems, interactions of sensuous with reflective and internal experience "produce" not inarticulate outpourings of feeling but a "poem," which is to say, language that does not merely articulate occurrences of feeling that are inarticulate in themselves, or communicate equally incommunicative empirical givens, but that represents these *as we perceive them*, i.e., shaped both by our active reception of and response to them: a "complex scene." Like the several other definitions of poetry in the "Preface" summarizing the mental actions detailed in the temporal processes of poetic production elaborated here, the non-empirical object at which, according to Wordsworth, the composed reality of "poetry" aims, the "worthy *purpose*," or moral and intellectual object, whose pursuit defines all poets worthy of the name, is what Wordsworth repeatedly calls neither "feelings," nor even "the representatives of feelings," "thoughts," but "knowledge." In contrast to his extensive definition of "poetry," Wordsworth's references to "knowledge" are, like the poetic language he uses and commends, strikingly direct. Yet, along with its subject and object, the kind of "knowledge" that Wordsworth has in mind he just as clearly leaves undefined. It is the complexity of experience these definitions articulate and Wordsworth's poetry represents that a poetics based in "real" rather than "poetic" "language" must address, if it, too, Wordsworth implies, is to aim at "knowledge," the "formally" unknown but "worthy purpose" of its object. For, like the specifically verbally enacted "power of judgment" Kant describes, Wordsworth's conception of the "knowledge" that any poem "worthy of the name" must afford is predicated upon the specific ability *to act linguistically*—that is, on the material *and* formally communicative basis proper to language alone. As intensely individual and subjective as it is extensive and social in attribution, at once dependent on and independent of experience, such a concretely linguistic condition of action, untraceable to any mechanical cause or precedent, expresses itself impersonally in the very act of uttering words. Even, as both Kant and Rousseau before him acknowledge, its own ("pre"-linguistic) basis must remain, by definition, definitively (i.e., linguistically) unidentifiable by any rigorous logical or causal account,[1] the performance or enactment of this condition composes a subject capable of describing, in a reciprocal, equal exchange of impersonal third-person pronouns with first ("it," "one"; "man," "I"), an experience of the world with which, because it is communicated in the common property of words, any and all subjects have the capacity to interact.

Still, without conflating and thus eradicating the differential development of "feeling" into "poetry," and of "poetry" into the "knowledge" that is its sole "worthy purpose" or end, it is difficult to square Wordsworth's definition of poetry, as product of unanticipated feeling replaced by "representative" "thoughts" repeated until they become "habits of mind" over time, with such pronouncements in the "Preface" as the following:

> What is a Poet? He is a man speaking to men; a man, it is true, endowed with more lively sensibility, more enthusiasm and tenderness, who has a greater knowledge of human nature . . .
> Poetry is the image of man and nature.
> Poetry is the most philosophic of all writing.
> Poetry is the breath and finer spirit of all knowledge . . .
> Poetry is the first and last of all knowledge—it is as immortal as the heart of man . . .
> I have said that poetry is the spontaneous overflow of powerful feelings:
> It takes its origin from emotion recollected in tranquillity; the emotion is contemplated till, by a species of reaction, the tranquillity gradually disappears, and an emotion, kindred to that which was before the subject of contemplation, is gradually produced, and does itself exist in the mind.[2]

Finally, when, in the "Essay Supplementary to the Preface," Wordsworth describes the pitfalls of officially arbitrated "taste,"

1. See Jean-Jacques Rousseau, *Discours sur les sciences et les arts; Discours sur l'origine et les fondements de l'inégalité parmi les hommes* (Paris: Flammarion, 1992 [Paris: Plissot, 1751]), pp. 199–209 esp. See Kant, *KU* B 68, X : 159–160.
2. Owen and Smyser, I: 138, 141, 149.

demonstrating, with reference to specific historical examples, that such poetasters succeed only in temporarily concealing lasting poetic merit, not only because all inculcated "taste" inevitably changes in time, but because taste itself is by definition *"creat[ed]"* by *"original"* writing itself[3] ("every author, as far as he is great and at the same time *original, has had the task of creating* the taste by which he is to be enjoyed"), he further links the unspecified notion, that poetry is "first and last of all knowledge," to the unnamed "power" produced by "great" authorship that he commends, yet does not, indeed, cannot elucidate, given its defining departure from known "habits" of thought.[4] Speaking of the need of the "reader" to "exert himself" in reading, to take part in the communication of creative "power" rather than "be carried" by the efforts of the poet "like a dead weight," the poet states: "Therefore to create taste is to call forth and bestow *power,* of which knowledge is the effect; and *there* lies the true difficulty."[5]

One could say that the "powerful feelings" with which Wordsworth's extensive definition of Poetry begins—and, as the narrative scope of that definition makes evident, *only* begins—end, for the poet, in a similarly familiar "romantic" trope, that of the feeling of "power" that Poetry itself bestows. But such a—metaphoric—transfer of powers would be inaccurate in Wordsworth's case. For while, on Wordsworth's view, poetic "originality" lies in an active, "creation" of "taste," and "to create taste is to . . . bestow power," "power" is, importantly, *not* the term with which his narrative account of the sole "worthy purpose" of poetry concludes. In an observation, to my knowledge, without precedent or parallel in the individual histories of poetics and philosophy, Wordsworth's copular statement equating the "creat[ion]" of "taste" with "bestow[ing] power," similarly extends *beyond* "power" to the direct

---

3. See this Chapter, n. 4 for full quote. For a strikingly similar view, expressed several decades later by an apparently radically dissimilar, equally "original" poet and theorist, with regard to the "sad politics!" ("triste politique!") of trying to prevent future "taste" from forming (in this case, the attempt to "gain a few years on M. Manet" by prohibiting the public exhibition of his "originality" in painting, see Mallarmé's great short essay "Le Jury de Peinture pour 1874 et M. Manet," in Penny Florence, *Mallarmé, Manet and Redon: Visual and Aural Signs and the Generation of Meaning* (Cambridge: Cambridge University Press, 1986), pp. 11–21 (19–21).

4. Owen and Smyser, III: 80 (emphasis in text).

5. Owen and Smyser, III: 82 (emphasis in text).

identification of "knowledge" as power's incomparable "effect." Rather than blithely equate feeling with poetry or power with knowledge (or even, and equally meaninglessly, knowledge with power), in the dogmatic manner of unthinking conflation enforced by more recent poetasters (themselves "furnish[ing] food for fickle tastes, and fickle appetites, of their own creation"[6]), Wordsworth understands that the "road" "shaped" by "every" "great and . . . *original*" "author"—the path in which poetry written in "real language" originates—leads to another in which real obscurity, "the true difficulty" "lies": that by which the experience of "power"—a sudden sense of the unmeasured or "irregular" carried by regular meter or measure—leads to the otherwise entirely unrelated experience of "knowledge" as its "effect."

One can say that the "true difficulty" of Wordsworth's poetic theory and "*purpose*" of his poetic practice lie "*there*" as well, in the difficulty of indicating what and where that elliptical "*there*"—the power of language to effect knowledge from its own "descriptive power"—is and may be found. For the main burden of Wordsworth's complex poetic theory—a burden consistently, one might say, almost reflexively, misread—owes to its attempt to elucidate and represent the "true difficulty" of producing, in language at once "philosophical" and "real," a "power" whose defining "purpose," "knowledge," can be identified neither with the "overbalance of pleasure" or "pain" of "excitement . . . carried beyond its bounds" that is its effect, nor with "the language really spoken by men," that, in the "co-presence of something regular," allows such an "irregular state of the mind" to persist. It is not the, in itself, senseless slogan, "knowledge" "is" "power," whether employed to liberatory or oppressive ends, but the absolutely critical and far more "difficult" categorical shift from "*power*" *to* "knowledge" that guides the "*purpose*" of poetry according to Wordsworth, a change in kind dependent upon our reading rather than rejecting the disturbance to habits of reading that such "power" effects, granting, therein, transmitted endurance to its verbally produced events.

How and if one *can* get from the here of "a complex scene" of interaction composed as much of "feeling" as of "thoughts," "act[ion]" as of "react[ion]," "sensations" as of "ideas," to a "*there*" constitutive of knowledge, is the question Kant answers in the theoretical–practical form of a mediating "power of judgment"—"bridge" or "transition" ("Übergang") between the non-communicating theoretical and

---

6. See Chap. 2, n. 5, this study.

practical "realms" of the First and Second Critiques. For, judgment, according to Kant, is a "power" defined equally by receptivity and action: the ability to experience "feeling" in sensing dynamic objects we do not know, and the "capacity" to externalize feeling into statements predicating those objects *not* as objects but as qualities ("it is beautiful," "it is sublime"). Kant calls this general ability to communicate, one that is neither subject- nor object-specific, "common sense."[7] While explicitly leaving the definition of its own origin, as innate or empirical, unexplored, Kant defines the practical operation of "common sense" as a verbal act rendering a noncognitive sense of an "object" ("it") "communicable," i.e., expressible by anyone "for everyone."

By contrast, Wordsworth's complex *poetics* of the "power" of "real language" seeks to represent, via the co-presence of "something regular," the course and content of disruptively powerful interactions with the real: to "effect," from those unprecedented experiences, "knowledge" both for the subject and reader of the poem. While Kant's subject of judgment, in short, is first constituted in the "free," verbal act of judging a perceived object "beautiful" or "sublime," not for itself but "for everyone," Wordsworth's poetry *represents* a subject experiencing the implicit loss of what, in the act of objective perception, it had assumed itself and subjectivity to be. It is to some of the most powerful of those representations that this analysis turn next.

7. See, in particular, Kant, *KU* B 65–69, X: 157–160. Kant's theory of judgment, and attribution of our ability to judge to the "condition" of "general communicability" he calls "common sense," is the central subject of the companion volume to this study, Brodsky, *The Linguistic Condition*.

Chapter 6

"Spontaneous Overflow" Staged

One of the most famous questions ever posed in poetry is the seemingly rhetorical one with which the narrative of the first modern epic in English poetic history properly begins: "... Was it for this/."[1] Initiating a question positioned alone at the end of an otherwise "regular" 10-beat line irregularly split here, however, into two unequal, textually separate halves, these four, thoroughly prosaic, monosyllabic words stand alone, isolated from their metrical complement by both a marked spatial break in the text and the period marking the full-stop conclusion of the extended sentence and unilaterally negative considerations that precede them:

This is my lot; ...
[...]
Unprofitably travelling toward the grave,
Like a false steward who hath much received
And renders nothing back.

Was it for this[2]

The strong medial caesura, falling after the sixth beat stress on "back," that forcefully divides the regular iambic pentameter line of which the graphically detached, "... Was it for this/," remains a part, appears to bring not only that individual line but the poet's entire narrative endeavor to the untimely conclusion it definitively pronounces itself: "And renders nothing back."[3] All of these elements serve to amplify the absolute impasse to which the poet's serially elaborated[4] attempts to

---

1. *The Prelude*, I: 269 [I: 272].
2. Ibid., I: 261–269.
3. Ibid.
4. *The Prelude*, I: 168–237 [I: 177–238].

"settle on some ... theme," by dint of "ambitious Power of choice" alone,[5] had led, the semantic dead-end attained by "days ... past/In contradiction"[6] till then.

The acknowledgement of a total inability to proceed, repeated, in distinctly Virgilian manner, across the defeated opening of this foundational epic poem, both previews the poem's climactic invocation and sublime description of "Imagination," as an autonomous external force of obstruction, in Book VI (1805 version)—"Imagination—lifting up itself/Before the eye and progress of my song/ ... I was lost as in a cloud"[7]—and issues immediately in the distinctively prosaic language the poet will use throughout this autobiographical epic to represent his own immediate experience of poetic action *internally* blocked: the sense, produced in the mind, of an "interdict" "hanging" on the "mind['s]" own "hopes"; the "hollow" quality not, as might be expected, of his openly avowed "ambition" as "Poet,"[8] but of the content meant to fill and substantiate that ambition, his "thought."[9] No longer "[a]

5. Again, the 1805 version describes that "ambitious Power of choice" in periphrastic, less directly impactful terms: "Sometimes, mistaking vainly (as I fear)/Proud spring-tide swellings for a regular sea, I ..."—the continuation of which is identical to the 1850 version: "settle on some British theme, some old/ Romantic tale told by Milton left unsung" (I: 177–180).

6. The 1805 version includes the, for this reader, far weaker account: "Thus from day to day/I live a mockery of the brotherhood/Of vice and virtue" (I: 238–240).

7. *The Prelude* [1805], I: 525–529.

8. *The Prelude*, I: 135 [I: 145].

9. "Hanging," "hopes," "hollow," "blank," "vacant," "soulless," and, of course, "thought" are all central terms of poetic action throughout Wordsworth and *The Prelude* in particular. For the poet's distinctive, repeated use of the verb "to hang"—fitting converse to his frequent use of "to move" and its substantive form, "motion"—see esp. *The Prelude* I: 330 [341]: "Oh! When I have hung/"; IV: 256 [248]: "As one who hangs down-bending from the side/"; V, ll. 381 [406], 398 [467], on the Boy of Winander: "Then sometimes, in that silence, while he hung/," and, soon thereafter, on the Boy's gravesite: "the grassy churchyard hangs/"; VI: 525–528 [453–456]), for the description of the "unveiled ... summit of Mont Blanc" as "a soulless image on the eye/That had usurped upon a living thought/That never more could be." Like "thought" and "thoughts," instances of "hope" and "hopes" are too frequent to be cited here. Readers of English romantic poetry will recognize the living legacy of many of these "prosaic" terms from pivotal passages in the works of Shelley and Keats as well.

discontented sojourner" of "the vast city," but "[f]ree as a bird to settle where I will," the poet may well see and state, "[t]he earth is all before me"[10] with regard to what lies ahead, yet, rather than effecting, let alone representing any "worthy" action engaged in upon the earth, he soon sees himself progressing, by very virtue of every self-thwarting effort he undertakes, toward the narrowest of earthly confinements instead, or, as he unsparingly describes, "in vain perplexity/Unprofitably travelling toward the grave." After expounding in great detail his search for the vehicle best "suit[ed]"[11] to his authorial "ambition"— whether to take up "some noble theme";[12] "settle" on a little-known ancient, "European"[13] or "British" one; unearth "some old Romantic tale by Milton left unsung";[14] "invent a tale" or "some variegated story" "from my own heart";[15] or "aspire" to "some philosophic song ... fitted to the Orphean lyre"[16]—and acknowledging midstream that, no matter the chosen topic nor how "lofty" its object, in each case "the insubstantial structure melts,"[17] Wordsworth short-circuits the prospect of future poetic action by proleptically reviewing "all" "the earth" that "is before me"[18] as mere space to be traversed en route "toward the grave," concluding the first half of Book One by renouncing poetry altogether:

> And ask no record of the hours, resigned
> To vacant musing, unreproved neglect
> Of all things, and deliberate holiday,
> Far better never to have heard the name
> Of zeal and just ambition, than to live
> Baffled and plagued by a mind that every hour

10. *The Prelude*, I: 9, 14 [I: 9–10, 15].

11. *The Prelude*, I: 221 [I:220]

12. *The Prelude*, I: 129 [I: 139]

13. *The Prelude*, I: 198 [I: 197]

14. *The Prelude*, I: 168–169 [I: 179–180]

15. *The Prelude*, I: 221–224 [I: 220–224]

16. *The Prelude*, I: 228–233 [I: 229–234]

17. *The Prelude*, I: 225. Again, the 1850 version improves in strength, compactness, precision, polysyllabic alliterative effect and originality of conception on the somewhat hackneyed paraphrase for heights toppled provided in 1805: "Lofty, with interchange of gentler things./But deadening admonitions will succeed/ ..." (1: 224–225 [1805]).

18. *The Prelude*, I: 14.

Turns recreant to her task; takes heart again
Then feels immediately some hollow thought
Hang like an interdict upon her hopes.
This is my lot; for either still I find
Some imperfection in the chosen theme,
Or see of absolute accomplishment
Much wanting, so much wanting in myself,
That I recoil and droop, and seek repose
In listlessness from vain perplexity,
Unprofitably travelling toward the grave,
Like a false steward who hath much received
And renders nothing back.

                    Was it for this
That one, the fairest of all rivers, loved
To blend his murmurs with my nurse's song,
[...][19]

Turning upon *this* "record" of "days . . . past [i]n contradiction"[20] by "a mind that every hour/Turns recreant to her task," the poet replaces "nothing" with an apparently rhetorical question, the near anacoluthon, or *projected* negation of a negation, posed by the now celebrated question: "Was it for this?" Based on the *absence* of a past affirmation, the powerful rhetorical effect of the poet's question, second perhaps only to Hamlet's in its impact upon the history of English verse, derives entirely from the impossible negative of a missing positive it posits, a "nothing" that, by definition, its own expression cannot enact (e.g., one must be in order to ask "not to be"), but, instead, far more powerfully

19. *The Prelude*, I: 252–271 [I: 254–273, 1805]. Its sole instances of alteration limited to the replacement of "given up" (I: 254 [1805]) by "resigned" in line 252, and the substitution of a comma for a dash in the punctuation of line 264 (I: 266 [1805]), Wordsworth's final 1850 version of this turning point, in Bk. I, is virtually identical to its predecessor in 1805, indicating that the poet's own *enactment* of his autobiographical epic's origin, in an open-ended question directed, as if on behalf of the external world, of himself, is one that remained a model of "what the Poet does" for him.

20. *The Prelude*, I: 237–238. This powerfully concise account of time passing on as the mind "recoils" to a standstill within itself, is less effectively, euphemistically rendered in the 1805 version cited in n. 6, this Chapter.

implies.[21] The logical discontinuity realized by the poet's abrupt question underscores why it appears rhetorical in the first place. For what that memorable question appears positively to negate, *rather than* question, is the absolute lack of relation, let alone equilibrium, between the poet, as agent acting within nature, able to "record" those actions with a certain "purpose" or "ambition" when he does, and the entirely impersonal, *non*-correspondent actions of nature itself.

By elegiacally lamenting the *absence* of his own ability to compensate, in poetic action, for nature's own, the poet indirectly implies the necessity of a correspondence between nature and himself, effectively positing a "B" (the subject as purposeful agent) predefined by its function as complement or counterpart to "A" (nature's impersonal acts), *yet* effecting this equivalence by first *negating* that "B" has fulfilled its part of that (subjectively projected) equation or exchange. The fact that "the fairest of all rivers," like all of nature, can only be attributed *by him* with any volition or ambition in his regard makes the task he sets himself, of righting that imbalance, as infeasible as preventing a figurative or imaginary "breeze" "felt *within*" to "correspond" to the "blessing," named in the opening of the poem, brought by the external "breeze" "blowing *on* my body," from "now becom[ing]/With quickening virtue," "A tempest, a redundant energy/Vexing its own creation."[22] The inexorable progress of a projected correspondence between inside and outside into a violent experience of their non-correspondence, as that of a "tempest" empowered by an internality in redundant relation with itself alone, is already represented in the entirely internal "[t]rances of thought and mountings of the mind" reported to "come fast upon me!" in the poem's first twenty lines, even as the poet incongruously asserts: "I cannot miss my way,"[23] just as it underlies the comparison drawn

---

21. The—literally—unprecedented nature of Wordsworth's abrupt question here is concretely realized in the earliest versions of *The Prelude*: the 150-line poem entitled simply "Was It For This," and the two-part 1799 text extending those 150 to 968 lines, both composed in Goslar in 1798 (the former, the only extant MS. of the poem written in Wordsworth's own hand, currently in the Wordsworth Library, Grasmere). Like the individual poem, "Was It For This," Part One of the 1799 Two-Part *Prelude* opens with the absolute anacoluthon, "Was it for this . . .," thus excluding any antecedent that might be understood as the referent of its opening deictic pronoun, "this" (l. 1). See *The Prelude: The Four Texts*, ed. Jonathan Wordsworth (London: Penguin, 1995), p. 8.

22. *The Prelude*, I: 34–38[I: 42–47] (emphasis added).

23. *The Prelude*, I: 18–20 [I: 19–21].

between "the Poet, gentle creature as he is" and "the Lover" in "his unruly times," on the basis of their shared inability to manage or compose their "own/Unmanageable thoughts."[24]

It is as if in response to that necessarily unanswerable question, of inestimable poetic recompense for lived experience that no nature ever requested, let alone sought, that the poet commences to recount what he will thereafter call the "story of my life".[25] Represented by the figure of "life" familiar from Dante, of a "road" whose course, composed in this case of *past* events, "lies clear before me,"[26] the image of the individual life as a linear path "of single and determined bounds"[27] attains to literal sense at the highpoint of the narrator's ensuing autobiographical "story" in Bk VI, the referential turning point not only of the Alps that the poet intends his path to cross but of the entire poem itself: "our future course, all plain to sight,/Was downwards . . . ."[28] As discussed in detail in Part II, Chapter 9 of this study, it is when a "future course" is indeed visible, but points in a direction directly contrary to the heights figuratively projected upon the landscape by the travelers themselves, that no further narrative concatenation of events but rather the profound rupture of narration takes place, and "that awful Power," "Imagination," instead rises "unfathered" "from the mind's abyss," preventing poet and poem not only from continuing on but constituting any "course" of action at all: "I was lost/Halted without an effort to break through."[29]

Yet, between the abrupt, apparently rhetorical question with which the autobiographical narrative of the poem begins—"Was it for this . . ."—and the interruption of that "life" "story" by the invocation of a "Power" of "Imagination" "so called/Through sad incompetence of human speech" in Bk. VI,[30] the intervening, represented events whose "single and determined bounds" align *with each other* to a remarkable extent, are anything but linear in their *narrative* interrelation; vividly

24. *The Prelude*, I: 135–139 [I: 145–149].

25. *The Prelude*, I: 639 [I: 667].

26. *The Prelude*, I: 640 [I: 667].

27. *The Prelude*, I: 641 [I: 669].

28. 1850 edn: VI: 684–685.

29. *The Prelude*, VI: 596–597. Cf. "I was lost as in a cloud,/Halted without a struggle to break through" (VI: 529–530 [1805]).

30. *The Prelude*, VI: 592–594. Cf. "Imagination—lifting up itself/Before the eye and progress of my song/Like an unfathered vapour, here that power/ . . ." (VI: 525–527 [1805]).

clear, indeed nearly homologous in their internal structural description, they are anything but "clear" in the diachronic "course" of their development. In addition, over and over again, or, as the poet states, "many a time,"[31] these events are narrated not as singular but as repetitive occurrences, each setting up a "scene" of action in which something disconcertingly out of the ordinary is made, perceived and felt to take place within the context of otherwise ordinary circumstances, not once and for all, in the classically progressive narrative sense, but some indefinite number of times in a past without certain end:

> [...]*[s]ometimes* it befel
> In these night wanderings, that a strong desire,
> O'erpowered my better reason [...][32]

Oh! when I *have hung* ... But ill-sustained[33]

> [...] not in vain
> By day or star-light thus from my first dawn
> Of childhood *didst* thou intertwine for me
> The passions that build up our human soul
> [...]
> [...] *In November days,*
> *When,* by the margin of the trembling lake,
> Beneath the gloomy hills, homeward *I went*
> In solitude, such intercourse was mine;
> Mine was it in the *fields both day and night,*
> And by the waters, *all the summer long*[34]

> [...] *and oftentimes*
> *When* we had given our bodies to the wind [...][35]

> Unfading *recollections!* at this hour
> The heart is almost mine with which *I felt*
> *From some hill-top on sunny afternoons,*

31. *The Prelude*, I: 298 [I: 291]
32. *The Prelude*, I: 317–318 [324–325] (emphasis added)
33. *The Prelude*, I: 330–333 [I: 341–344] (emphasis added)
34. *The Prelude*, I: 404–424 {{I: 431–451] (emphasis added)
35. *The Prelude*, I: 452–453 [478–479] (emphasis added)

The paper kite high among fleecy clouds
Pull in her rein like an impetuous courser,
Or from the meadows sent on gusty days
Beheld her breast the wind, then suddenly
Dashed headlong, and *rejected* by the storm.[36]

What ultimately "bef[alls]" the poet-narrator at each of these and other iterative moments he recounts is, in the poet-theorist's words, "the spontaneous overflow of powerful feeling": the experience of a power that, not limited to any necessarily delimited visible phenomenon in itself, can only be figuratively represented as something equally invisible—a "feeling" or "motion" felt to exceed or "flow" "over" an imagined boundary or line dividing what is containable from what is not containable within the mind. The vivid narratives of events in which such "powerful feeling" is repeatedly brought about all tell the story of a subject's active staging of "a scene" in which voluntary bodily movements on his part permit otherwise imperceptible motions on the world's part to appear, motions which transgress any expectation of containment and with it, the correspondence between understanding and experience that such containment enables. For it is that guiding sense of correspondence with an outside that permits the boy to use his own body to stage "scenes" of action within the world in the first place: to strap it to "steel" skates[37] or a horse that can augment its own power of motion; to steal a boat allowing him to "row,/Proud of his skill," while keeping his eyes fixed on an unmoving external "summit";[38] to "hang,"[39] whether from "slippery rock" "[a]bove", "almost (so it seemed)/ Suspended by the blast wind that blew amain";[40] or "down-bending from the side/ Of a slow-moving boat";[41] and to "bl[o]w mimic hootings to … silent owls"[42] by first fashioning together, "fingers interwoven,"[43] his own most natural, corporal mode of extension, his hands, into a

36. *The Prelude*, I: 491–498 [I: 517–524] (emphasis added)
37. *The Prelude*, I: 433 [I: 460]
38. *The Prelude*, I: 367–368, 370 [I: 396, 399]
39. *The Prelude*, I: 330, 338 [I: 341, 347], IV: 256 [IV: 247]; "hang" similarly figures prominently in the account of the Boy of Winander; see V: 381, 392 [V: 406, 417].
40. *The Prelude*, I: 331–334 [I: 342–345]
41. *The Prelude*, IV: 256–257 [IV: 247–248]
42. *The Prelude*, V: 373 [V: 398].
43. *The Prelude*, I: 370 [I 395].

single resounding "instrument" of imitation.[44] And it is precisely that sense of correspondence—the "for" linking "it" with "this" in "Was it for this," and which, that question implies, stands for nature's own imputed expectation of compensation from the poet for whatever actions it, just as imputedly, performed "for" him—that the progress of these "scenes," from the very first, destroys:

> [. . .] Ere I had told
> Ten birth-days, when among the mountain slopes
> Frost, and the breath of frosty wind, had snapped
> That last autumnal crocus, 'twas my joy
> With store of springes o'er my shoulder hung
> To range the open heights where woodcocks run
> Along the smooth green turf. [. . .]
>   [. . .] moon and stars
> Were shining o'er my head. I was alone
> And seemed to be a trouble to the peace
> That dwelt among them. Sometimes it befell
> In these night wanderings, that a strong desire
> O'erpowered my better reason, and the bird
> Which was the captive of another's toil
> Became my prey; and when the deed was done
> I heard breathings coming after me, and sounds
> Of indistinguishable motion, steps
> Almost as silent as the turf they trod.[45]

The iterative act of transgression these early lines represent as if it were occurring still, i.e., in past but nonetheless real and present time, forms the template for the encounters with nature for which the entire *Prelude* is perhaps best known. In each case something like a "strong desire" moves or "o'erpowers" the boy to cross a boundary of which he is consciously aware—here, the intellectual line of labor dividing all other "woodcocks" at "run" from "the captive of another's toil"—and the direct aftermath of such an overweening action is the experience of his own capacity for action, let alone ambition, transgressed, as the same nature that served as grounds for the "scene" of pursuit and usurpation he himself has set seems instead to have set itself in "motion," indeed to be actively pursuing or "com[ing] after" him. Reported here to take the boy

44. *The Prelude*, I: 372 [I: 397].
45. *The Prelude*, I: 306–325 [I: 310–332].

by surprise, this profound disruption of his own grounding within the world is one that, in a different "scene" described a few lines later, the boy purposefully employs his own body to stage:

> [. . .] Oh! When I have hung
> Above the raven's nest, by knots of grass,
> And half-inch fissures in the slippery rock
> But ill-sustained, and almost (so it seemed)
> Suspended by the blast that blew amain,
> Shouldering the naked crag, oh, at that time
> While on the perilous ridge I hung alone,
> With what strange utterance did the loud dry win
> Blow through my ear! The sky seemed not a sky
> Of earth—and with what motion moved the clouds![46]

The precarious act of hanging "ill-sustained" allows the boy to use the gravitational pull of his proximity to the earth to experience his own weight instead "suspended by" an invisible counterforce, that of "the blast that blew amain," and, in that ungrounded position, to experience the world not as a manipulable "scene" or platform for action but an unknown "earth" to which neither gravity, nor ground, nor their visible limit, "sky," pertain, and the "strange utterance" of the "loud dry wind" is not so much heard by, but impossibly "blow[s] through [his] ear" instead, his mind—limit or "sky" of the grounding or surface contact with the earth supplied by the senses—now seeming no longer a mind *of* man but mere corridor or funnel *for* "what motion moved the clouds!" That subjection to an invisible "motion" unknown, first experienced as a sensorily disassociative combination of "indistinguishable" "sounds" with "silent" "steps" after it "befell" the boy to appropriate another's "toil," takes on the visible, dramatic appearance of a "spectacle" of "huge and mighty forms" in the full-fledged narrative account of the stolen rowboat that follows, in short order, upon the scene of "hang[ing]" from the raven's nest just cited. Set off from the larger narrative as an independent story enclosed upon itself, the poet's representation of his experience, upon stealing a hidden rowboat, makes an otherwise prosaic youthful excursion into the occasion for one of the most perfectly realized individual narrative poems in English literature.

Between the episode of the stolen boat and the textual break following the exclamation, "and with what motion moved the clouds!"

---

46. *The Prelude*, I: 330–339 [I:341–350].

with which the raven's nest episode ends, the poet inserts the first of many non-narrative encomia of "immortal" "harmony"[47] that appear, without further explanation, after every radically discordant, "o'erpower[ing]" experience represented over the course of the poem: "Dust as we are, the immortal spirit grows/Like harmony in music, there is a dark/Inscrutable workmanship that reconciles/Discordant elements,/makes them cling together/In one society . . .[48] ["The mind of man is framed even like the breath/And harmony of music, there is a dark/Invisible workmanship that reconciles/Discordant elements and makes them move/In one society."[49]] Here giving "thanks" to "Nature" for the "means" "she"—not he!—has "deigned to employ . . . as best might suit her aim,"[50] while leaving unclear what Nature's "means" or "aim," with regard to such a willful act of self-suspension as he himself has just staged, might be, this self-disclaiming "praise" for "the calm existence that is mine"[51] appears to fill the experiential void and literal blank space to which the preceding scene of transgressive action and terrifying reaction has led, returning the poet to solid narrative footing again. Yet, in rejoining the "clear path" purportedly prescribed to him by his memory of past events, it is to water, and the theft of a vessel to cross it, to which the poet turns next, even as he ascribes to nature the volitional act of having first "led" him to that place. After yet another

47. *The Prelude*, I: 341 [I: 352].

48. *The Prelude*, I: 340–344.

49. *The Prelude*, I: 351–355 [1805].

50. *The Prelude*, I: 351–356. The lengthy circumlocution, in the 1805 version, of the concise attribution to "Nature," in the 1850 version, of his own act of daring to "employ" her "means" as he will, is distended across nine lines instead: "Praise to the end—/Thanks likewise for the means!—But I believe/That nature, oftentimes, when she would frame/A favoured being, from his earliest dawn/Of infancy doth open out the clouds/As at the touch of lightening, seeking him/With gentlest visitation, not the less,/Though haply aiming at the self-same end,/Does it delight her sometimes to employ/ [. . .]" (I: 361–369 [1805]). This early mention of a "lightening" flash, importantly employed to image the sudden eruption of "Imagination" upon consciousness, "when the light of sense goes out," at Simplon (I: 534–535 [1805]), or at the unexpected noonday "flash" of the "light" of the "moon" upon Snowdon (XIII: 39–41 [1805]), is similarly abbreviated and complicated by its ascription in 1850 to those "visitings" of "Nature" "[t]hat came with soft alarm," continuing: "like hurtless light/Opening the peaceful clouds . . ./" (I: 353–354 [1850]).

51. *The Prelude*, I: 349–350 [I: 360–361].

spatial break separating his encomium of a "calm existence" itself nowhere in evidence outside its own hymn-like "praise," the poet's singularly extended representation of a particular rather than iterative event begins with the prosaic statement of the individuality of this particular "act of stealth":

> One summer evening (led by her) I found
> A little boat tied to a willow tree
> Within a rocky cave, its usual home,
> Straight I unloosed her chain, and stepping in
> Pushed from the shore. It was an act of stealth
> And troubled pleasure, nor without the voice
> Of mountain echoes did my boat move on,
> Leaving behind her still, on either side,
> Small circles glittering idly in the moon,
> Until they melted all into one track
> Of sparkling light. [...]/[52]

Despite his parenthetical self-disclaimer, the singular agent of these vividly detailed events is their first-person narrator himself, and, like the "chain[ed]" boat "unloosed" by his actions alone, the acts and experiences he narrates constitute an entirely detachable poem within the poem: a fully formed dramatic representation, complete with peripeteia and enduring change, of what the "it" of the retrospective query, "Was it for this," might encompass within itself. For the visible line "[o]f sparkling light," made of "small circles . . . melted all into one track," in which the fluid surface beneath and "behind" the boat shows reflected the extending spatial interval his "act of stealth" has traversed, corresponds perfectly to the formation of "the road," connecting separate eddying incidents, of "the story of my life"[53] of which it is a part: a narrative that "lies plain before me" precisely because it is made of events enacted and experienced in the past.

---

52. *The Prelude.*, I: 357–367. The 1805 version is identical except for the linear, sentential and spatial break by which it separates this initial description off from the rest of the text, cutting it off at its concluding period punctuation, following "light," and continuing, two spatial lines later, not with "But," but with two additional lines of description, before describing himself as "one who proudly rowed" (see I: 394–397 [1805]).

53. *The Prelude*, I: 639–640 [I: 667–668].

That apparently seamless fusion, "into one track," of actions past with their present narration is counteracted within the poem, however, by another "unswerving line" of sight, one "fixed" in place, not by the visible trace of physical effort expended, whose "sparkling" watery "track" is soon to be effaced by the same physical laws that brought it about, but instead by the mind of the boy himself. For this is a boy who, having "chosen" the "point" toward which he directs the small craft he "rows" and his own "skill" in doing so, divides himself, so to speak, in two subjects—one moving toward a visible goal in space, the other fixing his view upon another point demarcating instead the "utmost boundary" of the earth's own visibility, the "horizon" within which this entire narrative scene is framed. The description of the watery "track" his efforts leave in their wake is immediately succeeded in the narrative by a contrary focus on what lies ahead and above:

> Of sparkling light. But now, like one who rows,
> Proud of his skill, to reach a chosen point
> With an unswerving line, I fixed my view
> Upon the summit of a craggy ridge
> The horizon's utmost boundary; far above
> Was nothing but the stars and the grey sky.[54]

Carried as much by a stolen vessel as by pride in "his skill" ("lustily/I dipped my oars into the silent lake") as he moves with a distinctly sexual momentum likened to that of Jove's rapacious "swan" ("And, as I rose upon the stroke, my boat/Went heaving through the water like a swan;/[…]") the boy suddenly sees the "silent lake" and still visible parameters of action he has set for himself forcibly usurped:

> [. . .] like a swan;
> When, from behind that craggy steep till then
> The horizon's bound, a huge peak, black and huge,
> As if with voluntary power instinct
> Upreared its head. I struck and struck again,
> And growing still in stature the grim shape
> Towered up between me and the stars, and still,
> For so it seemed, with purpose of its own
> And measured motion like a living thing,

54. *The Prelude*, I: 367–372 [I: 394–400].

Strode after me. With trembling oars I turned,
And through the silent water stole my way
[…][55]

Rather than "indistinguishable sound" or invisible "motion," what the
boy perceives here is a fully embodied "spectacle" "with purpose of its
own,"[56] "[o]f unknown modes of being"[57] in "measured motion," "huge
and mighty forms, that do not live/Like living men"[58] and whose visible
pursuit of him erase all known "familiar shapes" and "pleasant images"[59]
from his mind:

[…] after I had seen
That spectacle, for many days, my brain
Worked with a dim and undetermined sense,
Of unknown modes of being, o'er my thoughts
There hung a darkness, call it solitude
Or blank desertion. No familiar shapes
Remained, no pleasant images of trees,
Of sea or sky, no colours of green fields,
But huge and mighty forms, that do not live
Like living men, moved slowly through the mind
By day, and were a trouble to my dreams.

Wisdom and Spirit of the universe!
Thou Soul that art the eternity of thought
[…].[60]

Before the poet replaces the terrifying events and advent of "real"
poetics ("with purpose of its own and measured motion") he has
experienced and narrates with another, narratively disconnected
encomium to an "eternity" of "wisdom and spirit" not his, he describes
an interaction in nature in which he sees and experiences himself
overcome: a "spontaneous overflow of powerful feeling" staged and

55. *The Prelude*, I: 376–386 [I: 404–413].

56. *The Prelude*, I: 391, 386 [I: 398].

57. *The Prelude*, I: 393 [I: 420].

58. *The Prelude*, I: 384, 397–398 [I: 411, 425–426].

59. I*The Prelude*, I: 395–396. Cf.: "No familiar shapes/Of hourly objects,
images of trees …" (I: 411, 422–423 [1805]).

60. *The Prelude*, I: 390– 402 [I: 417–429].

undergone as overpowering "scene." This is a scene of action traversing the natural world no less than the mind itself, in which "powerful feeling" is represented in the prose of "huge and mighty forms" capable of acting upon the subject whose actions bring them about. Both visible *and* internal to him, "seem[ing]" first to "str[i]de after [him]" and, when no longer externally perceptible, "to move slowly through [his] mind" instead, these abruptly appearing forms make the mind itself no less than nature itself, i.e., mind and nature extending as far and further than the eye can see, into equivalent, delimited containers—landscapes, chambers or theaters—traversed by visible and invisible actions without end. The collision of these "measured" forms of force, or "real poetics," is perhaps most effectively represented by the merely apparently contradictory description, "no colours of green fields," in which the poet literally parses the worth of words themselves by dividing the word for a category of visual sensation ("colours") from one of the visual sensations ("green") it names, making "green" name instead the present absence of "green"—a not only sayable, but complexly meaningful, while objectively insensible, prosaic phrase. The stated negation of the experience of the "colour" of a "familiar," visible embodiment of color, even as that color and its customary embodiment are referred to as one—"green fields"—has the countereffect of making *the words*, "colour" and "green," take on an active, nearly thingly quality, the names themselves acting more like independent substances than the designations for qualities thereof. Here the poetic staging of a scene of interaction makes language active itself, as the intentional "fix[ing]" of a limit of vision—like that of any conventionally applicable prosaic term to an object or event—is transgressed by an ongoing physical motion, akin to "regular" metrical language, undertaken at the same time.

The motion of "huge and mighty forms" appearing forcefully to contradict his own, much like a "green field" flatly described to appear to have "no colour" at all, is produced by the inverse action, of a willful *cessation* of "rapid" motion on the boy's part, in the skating episode narrated next. Like the others in the string of scenes of "overflow" whose staging and experience are represented in Book I—acts of representation undertaken in response to the poet's own unanswerable, "Was it for this," that attempt to predicate, in words equal in "real" "use" value to "it," the personal experience of an impersonal power that "all poems to which any value can be attached" make available in and for "thought"—the magnificent narration of "wheeling about," "proud and exultant," on appended blades of "steel," that next appears within the poem follows upon another disconnected interval of self-disclaiming commemorative verse, this time celebrating the general "Wisdom and Spirit of the universe" for "sanctifying" and "purifying thus/The elements of feeling and of thought" "for me,"[61] not "[o]ne summer evening," but "all the summer long."[62] After a further spatial break, the poem, however, recommences "in" both another season and an entirely different, vividly detailed, episodic narrative vein:

> And in the frosty season, when the sun
> Was set, and visible for many a mile
> The cottage windows blazed through twilight gloom,
> I heeded not their summons: happy time
> It was indeed for all of us—for me
> It was a time of rapture! Clear and loud
> The village clock tolled six,—I wheeled about,
> Proud and exulting like an untired horse
> That cares not for his home. All shod with steel,
> We hissed along the polished ice [. . .]
> [. . .]
> And not a voice was idle; with the din
> Smitten the precipices rang aloud;
> The leafless trees and every icy crag
> Tinkled like iron, while far distant hills
> Into the tumult sent an alien sound
> Of melancholy not unnoticed. . .
> [. . .]
> Not seldom from the uproar I retired
> Into a silent bay, or sportively
> Glanced sideway, leaving the tumultuous throng,
> To cut across the reflex of a star
> That fled, and, flying still before me, gleamed
> Upon the glassy plain . . .[63]

That "sideway" slide or "glance" separates the boy not only from the "uproar" of "voice" and "ring[ing]" "precipice" alike but from the natural course of the physical laws by which vision follows light, as he instead "cut[s] across" the line of light or "reflex of a star" his own motion ("that fled . . . before me") defined. The acceleration of motion provided by

61. *The Prelude*, I: 401, 410– 412 [I: 428, 437– 439].

62. *The Prelude*, I: 424 [I: 451].

63. *The Prelude*, I: 425–452 [I: 452–478].

sharpened steel "flying . . . [u]pon the glassy plain" causes two "line[s] of motion," otherwise extending in tandem, to intersect, and reveal the dynamics of transgression that, feeding upon themselves, fuel the boy's "rapture," and form the basis for the "show-stopping" scene to come. For in this instance, the boy, having achieved a critical, "spinning" speed, abruptly exerts the commensurate opposite force required to "stop" himself in his tracks, thereby making the world appear to "wheel by [him]" instead. Willfully, forcibly disrupting his own artificially accelerated motion upon the surface of the earth, the boy effectively renders sensible the insensible rotation of the earth itself, a turning motion no subject whose ground it is can perceive:

> . . .and oftentimes,
> When we had given our bodies to the wind,
> And all the shadowy banks on either side
> Came sweeping through the darkness, spinning still
> The rapid line of motion, then at once
> Have I, reclining back upon my heels,
> Stopped short; yet still the solitary cliffs
> Wheeled by me—even as if the earth had rolled
> With visible motion her diurnal round![64]

Rather than "troubl[ing] [his] dreams at night," the "visible motion" with which the "solitary cliffs" "[b]ehind me did . . . stretch in solemn train," appears to the boy who "stood and watched . . . tranquil as a dreamless sleep."[65] Whether unnaturally "tranquil" or terrifying, the experience each of these individual stagings of contradictory motion describes is one in which the "familiar shapes"[66] of the things we perceive in nature are erased, the relations that enable their perception actively disrupted, upended. Narrating empirical actions and their experience in the active language really used by men, those "scenes" *are* prosaic representations *of* the "spontaneous overflow of powerful feeling," the sense of an uncontainable internal motion that those actions, like the "real language" of any "poetry" worthy of the name, effect. They are, in the words of the poet-theorist, "what the Poet does"; and "what" they produce "is" what "Poetry is . . .". For these "scenes" are where the complexity of the poet's most cited, least read definition of "Poetry" *and*

64. *The Prelude*, I: 453–460 [I: 478–486].
65. *The Prelude*, I: 460–463 [I: 486–489].
66. *The Prelude*, I: 395 {{I: 422].

the "complex" actions and interactions his poetry represents meet: where the scenography of an autobiography represents theory in practice.

It does so because the "boy" subject of these "scenes" stages *and* participates in them himself, using his own body as a means to compose and enact them, therein effecting the kind of empirically contingent, intellectual action that, Wordsworth states, the "Poet does": "consider man and the objects that surround him as acting and re-acting upon each other, so as to produce an infinite complexity of pain and pleasure." The "man" whom "the Poet," *writing as subject*, "considers," however, is himself, "acting and re-acting" "upon" "the objects that surround him," and the "infinite complexity" of feeling that "the Poet," having "thought long and deeply," "produces" within the reader is "representative" of that which the subject and composer of these "scenes" actively produces in himself. Just as many of the "scenes" themselves are iterative rather than staged and undergone once and for all, and all share a common dynamic of transgressing "natural," subject–object relations of perception, so through the verbal act of *representing* repetitive actions *in situ* of which he himself is both agent and part, the Poet, writing as subject, "really" authors the interactive experience he "has" "really" used his body to produce. This subject acts in such a way as to perceive his own active staging of a "scene," of things and forces in correspondence with each other, suddenly exceeded by a kind of motion he can instead only undergo or "feel" instead, and, just as the occurrence of "a spontaneous overflow of powerful feeling" requires a composed, prosaic "scene" of representation within which to take place, the experience of uncontainable motions and corresponding emotions can only be memorialized by their "representatives" in "thought."

Each of these "scenes" of "powerful overflow" is delimited within the narrative itself; unmistakable in the "purpose," of making a certain power perceptible, that they delineate but never explain, each maintains its unsettling, narrative lucidity by never learning—in traditional narrative fashion—from previous experience, previous "scenes." Instead each is enacted and experienced anew, as if unremembered in the event, just as any "spontaneous" experience, by definition, must be, and much as our minds experience in encountering every individual poem.

Part II

"Real Language" in Action

Chapter 7

"Strange Fits"

Of the many pivotal narratives in Wordsworth's poetry of "real language" that put "the true difficulty" of his poetic principles to the test, two "experiments"—as Wordsworth calls them[1]—from the *Lyrical Ballads* (1800) represent the passage from "power" to "knowledge" as a profound experience of discontinuity inhering in the very pursuit of "something regular" itself. Most importantly, Wordsworth renders that experience *articulate*, relating internal feeling and perceived "scene" through the least phenomenal form of externalization, the concrete "fit" of line and content occurring only, as Kant states in the *Logik*,[2] in the "concretely constructed" "things" of geometry. While the sight lines of our perspective upon it are naturally geometrical in their own formation, Nature, as the poet discovers, proves no such delimited "thing" in our purposeful interaction with it, and the "image

---

1. Owen and Smyser, "Advertisement" to the *Lyrical Ballads*, I: 116.

2. See Chap. 2, n. 19. In the *Logik,* Kant divides the "things" we ourselves make "*in concreto*" and thus can "define" in "real" rather than merely "nominal" terms, from all the experiential sensory phenomena we instead perceive in *a priori* delimited, representational–cognitive form. Most importantly for Wordsworth's poetics, on a par with the nonphenomenal, purely logical "constructions" delineated in the empirically noncontingent forms of "geometry," and the "free" (or undelimited), similarly noncontingent actions he calls "moral things" or "matters" ("Sachen der Moral"), Kant defines "what one understands under a word" ("was man unter einem Wort versteht") as uniquely available to "real definition." In Wordsworth, the subject's active staging of geometrically delineated "scenes" of sensory experience, in tandem with undertaking dynamic trajectories of motion, repeatedly brings the "familiar images" of delimited representational knowledge and the "motions" of unknown "mighty forms" (or, as we shall see, "thoughts") into violent conflict.

of man and nature"[3] that, Wordsworth states, "Poetry is," must be brought into being not pictorially or figuratively, i.e., as *individual* "image" in the traditional, static sense, but through the representation of the changing interrelation and interaction (the "and") conjoining "man and nature" over time. As little a "nature poet" as self-centric "romantic," Wordsworth, the "real language" poet, produces an "image of man and nature" that is necessarily narrative in nature. Before turning to some of the especially sceno-graphic narratives in the *Lyrical Ballads*, in which geometry and the temporality of human experience are represented to collide, Wordsworth's theoretical account of "what" "the Poet" "*does*" to compose such "scene[s]" bears repeating:

> What then does the Poet? He considers man *and* the objects that surround him as acting and re-acting upon each other, so as to produce an infinite complexity of pain and pleasure; he considers man in his own nature and in his ordinary life as contemplating this with a certain quantity of immediate knowledge, with certain convictions, intuitions, and deductions, which from habit acquire the quality of intuitions; he considers him as looking upon this *complex scene of ideas and sensations*, and finding everywhere objects that immediately excite in him sympathies which, from the necessities of his nature, are accompanied by an over-balance of enjoyment.[4]

The interdependence of narration and image, or active verb and object, indicated in this description of the Poet's already *representational* "consideration" of man—"*as* acting and re-acting" with "the objects that surround him"; "*as* looking upon a complex scene" composed equally of "ideas and sensations"—is concretely realized in one of Wordsworth's most celebrated "Lucy poems": a traditional, alternating six- and eight-beat ballad of alternating-rhyme, iambic quatrains, whose perfectly regular, formal repetition appears to join narration seamlessly with vision. "Strange fits of passion" not only narrates an event dependent upon "looking" but declares, in its eponymous opening line, the recurrence of such events throughout the speaker's past: "Strange fits of passion *have* I known," which is to say, with Wordsworth's "Preface" as crib: at undefined times in the past, I have come to "know" the "powerful feeling" or "irregular state of mind" that "[b]ut in the Lover's ear" (the poem continues) "I" now "will dare to tell." The ensuing, geometrically

---

3. Owen and Smyser, I: 141.
4. Owen and Smyser, I: 140 (emphasis added).

framed, step-by-step recounting of "[w]hat once to me befell" in the course of an otherwise regularly occurring action serves to demonstrate how regularity and irregularity come into conflict when anyone subject to the aspirations and expectations of a "Lover"—which is to say, any human subject whatsoever—employs nature as his plumb line in their pursuit.

The name of the speaker's aim in "Strange fits" is "Lucy," and as its speaker follows a familiar "path" to Lucy's cottage, his willing submission to the immediate sensation of "something regular"—the hoofbeats of the horse that carries him—allows him to focus another sense, his vision, upon a single, distant object, the "moon":

> When she I lov'd, was strong and gay
> And like a rose in June,
> I to her cottage bent my way,
> Beneath the evening moon.
>
> Upon the moon I fix'd my eye,
> All over the wide lea;
> My horse trudg'd on, and we drew nigh,
> Those paths so dear to me.[5]

Even as he "bent [his] way" by known "paths" toward the attainment of a known goal (Lucy's "cottage"), he "fix'd" his "eye," the speaker recounts, on an object so categorically removed from his own earthbound trajectory that no matter the distance eclipsed by his changing position in space, its proximity *to* him will not change. As the "climb[ing]"

---

5. Wordsworth, *Lyrical Ballads and Other Poems, 1797*–1800, ed. James Butler and Karen Green (Ithaca; Cornell University Press, 1992), pp. 161–162: "Strange fits of passion," ll. 5–12 (hereafter Butler and Green, followed by title of individual poem and numbers of lines cited). A helpful investigation of longstanding and contemporary debates surrounding the design of the so-called "Lucy poems" is offered by Mark Jones in, *The 'Lucy Poems': A Case Study in Literary Knowledge* (Toronto: University of Toronto Press, 1995). While noting that, before Arnold, Margaret Oliphant first established the five poems (written in Goslar Germany from 1798 to 1799) as a group, Jones reminds us that while Wordsworth himself remained unusually "silent" on their subject, "he still placed the poems in a way that suggested the grouping he did not create" (pp. 71, 6, 9).

movement toward his terrestrial object progresses, however, that celestial object appears to move in an arc inverting his own: "And now we reach'd the orchard-plot,/And, as we climb'd the hill,/Towards the roof of Lucy's cot/The moon descended still."[6] The combined experience of bodily ascent and the "fix[ing]" of vision extended from the body upon a discrete, "descend[ing]" object produces a complex kind of unconsciousness in the traveler: a "sweet dream" of countervailing movements mediated by a single, visible point. When, by its mere extension, this perceptible relation of inversion suddenly changes into an opposition, the one motion usurping rather than accompanying the other, the traveler's constant object—previously "fix'd" by the continuously graduating angles of vision directed at it from his own position—vanishes altogether from view. The poem continues:

> In one of those sweet dreams I slept,
> Kind Nature's gentlest boon!
> And, all the while, my eyes I kept
> On the descending moon.
> My horse mov'd on; hoof after hoof
> He rais'd and never stopp'd:
> When down behind the cottage roof
> At once the planet dropp'd.[7]

Even as the "path" pursued, "hoof after hoof," brings the traveler closer to his chosen goal, Lucy's abode, his external focal point on the way to that goal appears to disappear so suddenly as to seem "at once" to "drop" from view. The continuous coordination of point and movement by the poem's narrator, resulting in the eclipse of difference between them, collapses the visual field they delineated. For any visual field or plane upon which motion can be outlined is defined by axes to which a series of coordinates can be assigned, and what occurs when the interrelated bases of coordination become defunct is the departure, so to speak, of linear variables from the page. Looked at from another "angle," one necessarily unavailable, in real time, to the subject of "Strange fits," it is the intersection *within himself, as* subject, of two continuous but otherwise disconnected lines, or "path[s]," that renders the disappearance of one, and new-found terror of what lies or, rather, no longer lies, at the end of the other, inevitable. If ever there was a

---

6. Butler and Green, "Strange fits . . .," ll. 13–16.
7. Butler and Green, "Strange fits . . .," ll. 17– 24.

"visible scene"[8] conjoining "man"—subject of "passions," of "path[s]" of action, accidents of "dream" and absences of consciousness—with the ever-enticing, fully disinterested appearances of nature, the changing contours and felt contents of Wordsworth's lucid narrative of a fatal "fit" relates it. The "real" product of interactions between man and nature *and* "man and his own nature," the geometrically delineating "language" in which his speaker "tell[s]," as if plotting a figure, "what once to me befell," represents, moreover, the discontinuous plotline befalling, according to Wordsworth, all poetry "of … value." For, translating the sudden dissolution of a visual field first defined by the fixing of his vision into a subjunctive fatality as "real" as it is imaginary—"O, I cried, what if Lucy should be dead!"—the speaker's final exclamation "knows" no declarative answer but, indeed, an aftermath: this poem rendering the sudden experience of the *irregular* repeatable by its *regular* representation for posterity, namely a "strange fit of passion." The inclusion of the perceiving subject *within* a figure of its own progressive bodily delineation must include, in the course of its impassioned progress, the perfect coincidence, or "fit," of "something regular" and something "fix'd," or death.

Thus we can say that, in its own, active way, just as his "Preface" argues against the "contradistinction between Poetry and Prose," and for "the more philosophical one of Poetry and Matter of Fact, or Science,"[9] the aftermath of figuration that Wordsworth's poem so effectively, affectingly represents demonstrates—not by illustrative parable, but "in a language arising out of repeated experience and regular feelings"—the opposition between motion and identity underlying and undercutting all matters of facts, first canonized in Zeno's paradoxes. It is in the "real" and "far more philosophical language of Poetry," itself "the first and last of all knowledge," that Wordsworth communicates the cognitive incompatibility of position and motion, or point and line, by which "knowing" ("fixing" an identity to) the one occludes knowledge of the other. Like Zeno's exemplary Achilles and tortoise, or arrow in flight, or, for that matter, Bohr and Heisenberg's demonstrably, never knowably coincident light wave and particle, the representational paradox, of interactive stasis and motion, presented by Wordsworth's quotidian "complex scene" requires—and remains resolutely irresoluble in—time, just as, in his complex poetic theory, the fixed elements, or *verba*, and the "power" of "meter" that carries them "on," must remain mutually

8. *The Prelude*, V: 384 [V: 409].
9. Owen and Smyser, I: 141.

distinct from, even as they depend upon each other, if the advent of an actual *action* and experience of change is to be perceived to take place at all.

Yet in representing a first-hand *experience*, rather than exemplary demonstration, of a representational paradox, Wordsworth's poem presents a reality far more difficult than any theoretically conceived, physical model to parse. By maintaining a fixed position or point of leverage outside it, one may draw a line, straight or curved, from one set of coordinates to another, simply by calculating the values prescribed by the formula of a slope, just as one can draw or track a moving object's trajectory. Yet, in the poet's definitively non-theoretical account of such coordination, the fulcrum of delineation lies not in an external instrument or (immobile) prime mover but a *subject in motion* whose orienting reference point appears, from his perspective, to be moving as well. The description of a curve—in this case, the upward curve of the path to Lucy's cottage—in tandem with an external point is not traced here by a geometer similarly situated outside the figure so formed, but, rather, derives from a constantly changing sight line whose focus of vision remains "fixed." In short, rather than delineating a figure whose "identity" represents graphically a series of correspondences between number and line, Wordsworth's poem outlines two distinct series constituted only by the subject in whom they intersect. The regular movement of a weight-bearing body along a predefined trajectory on earth, and the weightless ability of an "eye" located within that body to "fix," as in a "dream," on a point forever separated from earth, cleave their single subject in two, as the plane of vision his actions created seems to fold upon itself, the "planet" whose arc of motion it contained abruptly appearing not only to have "dropp'd" from the picture but to have taken the picture frame with it.

As human plus horse power, or motivating feeling (here named "Lucy") and motive force, pass, like Zeno's arrow, to and through each measure of the prospective journey they successively create and destroy, the vector of the line they compose remains the same, for a cottage, and not the moon (or any other ungrounded body), is the traveler's known goal. Yet it is the visible moon, in its position above the vehicle to which his own impassive body is joined, that provides the constant counterpoint to this traveler "carried," to cite Wordsworth on "quiescent" "reader[s]," "like a dead weight." Constant in that it neither comes closer to, nor recedes further from him as he and horse "climb" "on," the apparent movement of the "descend[ing]" moon is as distinct from the traveler's actual ascent as is the imperceptible motion of the earth upon which he rides. The result of its sudden falling from view is the traveler's equally sudden internal fall, from "one of those sweet dreams" induced by an illusory continuity of the senses[10]—"Kind Nature's gentlest boon!"[11]—to equally unbidden "thoughts" of death: "What fond and wayward thoughts will slide/Into a Lover's head—/'O mercy!' to myself I cried,/'If Lucy should be dead!'"[12]

If the steady hoofbeat of his horse's advance combined with the "fix[ing]" of his vision endowed the traveler with a dream-like experience of Nature's beneficence—the blissful impression of a peaceful co-existence between infinitude and the finite, between ongoing experience and an objective *point de repère*, enjoyed by any "Lover"—the sudden contradiction of the one by the other that their very coordination brings, provides the opening or angle for another kind of direction and action, the bent of "wayward thoughts."[13]

For Lucy is not feared dead because the traveler sees her in the fallen moon; rather he sees his own seeing as dead, as an act no longer in

10. Such is the illusorily autonomous coordination of the senses positively attributed by Aristotle and others to an additional, equally physical, yet nonetheless purportedly supervisory "common sense." While the need for a supplementary organ of sense perception signaled by this conception indicates the insufficiency of notions of autonomous human sensation in the first place, it is precisely the dream of a specifically sensory overseer of the senses—of sensory experience somehow simultaneously governed by sensory experience, across a homogeneity of sensation reminiscent of tautology in discursive logic—that Kant's pathbreaking reconception of "common sense" as a specifically linguistic ability disrupts. I discuss the social and grammatical composition and real, practical consequences of this theoretical reconception in the companion volume to this study, *The Linguistic Condition*, Part. I, Chap. 2.

11. Butler and Green, "Strange fits . . .," ll. 17–18.

12. Butler and Green, "Strange fits . . .," ll. 25–28.

13. William Empson's important indication of the disparate meanings of "sense" in Wordsworth's work finds its counterweight in the poet's consistent use of the word "thoughts," perhaps the most regularly occurring and singularly enigmatic substantive named throughout the *corpus* of his poems. See, among many other decisive appearances of the term, the anti-climactic, if not directly contradictory final lines of the deeply emotive recollections of past sensory experiences composing the elegiac "Intimations Ode": "To me the meanest flower that blows can give/Thoughts that do often lie too deep for tears." Cf. William Empson, "Sense in the *Prelude*," in *The Structure of Complex Words*, Cambridge: Harvard University Press, 1989 [1st edn 1951], pp. 289–305.

correspondence with the objects it perceives. Vision and motion go together here; yet it is the "fix[ing]" of vision upon something outside the continuous path of motion that creates the ocular appearance of that thing's disappearance, and "slide[s]" into its place the "thought" of Lucy's death.[14] That "place" is now "in the Lover's head," rather than the heavens, and just as the speaker prefaces the poem by stating he "will dare to tell/But in the lover's ear alone,/What once to me befell,"[15] true to Wordsworth's poetic theory, the objective event retold in "Strange fits of passion" is at once enacted by the poem itself: the "wayward thoughts" described to enter "in the Lover's head" have now entered the "ear" of every "lover"—listener or reader—to whom the poem "bef[a]ll[s]," anyone whom it carries along the course of disrupted experience it powerfully describes. Similarly, the "thoughts" toward which the poet ultimately turns—"thoughts" in themselves untoward in that their object is not Lucy but her possible death—signal the disappearance from the face of the earth of that which only those who see the earth as face or surface can envision, a finite object that they alone, in their capacity as subjects, join to infinity. For whoever sees—or in any way senses—the empirical world in *articulate* form makes himself or herself the nexus or locus of intersection between objects and motion, constancy and continuous change, and when the latter obliterates the former, it is also he or she who notices.

In the same manner, every individual act of human sense perception, whether flawed or fictive in content, and purposefully, accidentally or mechanically produced, adds to the world another perspectival bridge from which the perceiver may sense, as in a "dream," the unification of things with movement. Acts of perception, we might say, are to the world of human events what the structures of snowflakes are to the world of natural events: ephemeral constellations embodying an unrepeatable register of continuously changing forces upon the matter in which they happen to coincide, forms that must achieve an equipoise of weight and content if they are to crystallize as forms at all. Yet, while matter resists and thus provides the medium for the imprint of external forces, human perception first takes place, most significantly, in the distinctively human *act* of conjoining these. And because perception adds to the world the bridges between things and non-things it makes,

14. For a similar view of the speaker's "thought" taking the place vacated by the moon, see Robert Marchant, *Principles of Wordsworth's Poetry* (Swansea: Brynmill Publishing Co., 1972), p. 45.

15. Butler and Green, "Strange fits . . .," l. 4.

forming the constellations of givens and conditions that, at any moment, inform our experience and understanding of the real, perception also carries with it its own destruction in time. As the single seat of both dynamic and object-specific experience that it alone has the nonnatural or, in Rousseau's terms, "moral or political"[16] power to coordinate, it is the human subject and forger of relations, who, in seeing them vanish, "should be dead" by the poem's end. Instead, "Strange fits of passion" states, "wayward thoughts" of something no longer living—"representatives" of "feelings" "past," to recall the "Preface"— enter into the speaker's head. The poet calls that something "Lucy," and "Lucy" having been the goal that first turned the speaker toward "familiar paths" now turned "wayward" and inward with contradiction, indeed he may just as well. For, just as "Lucy" remains as elusive an historical identity as identifiable presence in the poems traditionally related under her name,[17] so the "true difficulty" involved in representing "Lucy," or whatever, for Wordsworth, that name for "light" represents, may have more to do with the poet's view of the "worthy" "purpose" defining all poetry—the challenge, met only in the "real language of men," of arriving at "knowledge" from "power"—than with a specific object of affection feared "dead."

For what dies in "Strange fits of passion" is Wordsworth's theory of the life of poetry itself, that of a continuous "co-presence of something regular" able to "throw a sort of half-consciousness of insubstantial existence over the whole composition,"[18] the very sort of absence of thought into which the horse's measured hoofbeats lull the traveler and the regular beat of his poetic meter lulls the poet's reader. And what lives for Wordsworth is that theory as well, the theory of "thoughts" that "will" enter into any "Lover's head," i.e., any impassioned subject of perception who experiences, whether in the world or in words, the interaction between a continuous, enabling state of "half-consciousness" and the disabling—unanticipated or "spontaneous"—eruptions of

16. Rousseau employs the term in opposition to "physical" or natural capacities and "needs" in the Second Discourse and elsewhere. See Rousseau, *Discours sur l'origine et les fondements de l'inégalité parmi les hommes*. Paris: Flammarion, 1992 [orig. pub. 1751; 1755]. p. 267; *Essai sur l'origine des langues, où il est parlé de la mélodie et de l'imitation musicale*. Ed. Charles Porset. Paris: Nizet, 1969 [orig. pub. 1781; written 1740s?, 1750s?], Chap. 3.

17. See this Chapter, n. 5.

18. Owen and Smyser, I: 147.

"powerful feeling" to which, with duration, dream-like states inevitably tend. Such "thoughts" do not accompany and "temper" the "overbalance" of feeling experienced by a subject "climb[ing]" toward a determined goal, but occur when, in the course of that approach, the relations composing the subject's steadying perceptions are forcefully interrupted by the angle of pursuit itself. Such disruption, in turn, not only makes the speaker's purported purpose suddenly appear unattainable, permanently out of reach, but to have been rendered a "dead" letter in the moment its identification as determining motivation had been made.[19]

Yet one may ask whether it is the purpose of the goal-oriented activity narrated in "Strange fits of passion" or, rather, the unforeseen interruption of that activity the speaker undergoes, that indeed embodies or represents the "worthy purpose" at which, as Wordsworth asserts, the user of "prosaic" language whom that same language calls "poet" must aim. For, whoever or whatever "Lucy" may be is reported either to disappear or to have already disappeared in the course or at the outset of each of these posthumously grouped, eponymously entitled poems. Is the "purpose" of the "poet" "worthy of the name," in short, embodied in "Lucy"'s presence or in her absence? In at least one "Lucy" poem, the difference between the two emerges not by way of their narrative separation, steady coordination, and abrupt disruption—the progressive stories of expectations upended so central to Wordsworth's poetics overall—but in their own poetic representation and placement side by side, in two stanzas separated only by space and verbal tense. Interruption is, incongruously, the *ongoing* suspension of action of the "Lucy" poem in which the "thought" said to have "slid" abruptly into the poet's "head" in "Strange fits of passion" is represented not only as already realized but as an entirely material, immutable reality, and, as such, "now" and interminably projected beyond itself.

19. Owen and Smyser, I: 146.

Chapter 8

"A Slumber . . ."

The "[s]he" of this most well-known "Lucy" poem begins and remains pointedly unnamed, "a thing."

> A slumber did my spirit seal,
>   I had no human fears:
> She seem'd a thing that could not feel
>   The touch of earthly years.
>
> No motion has she now, no force;
>   She neither hears nor sees:
> Roll'd round in earth's diurnal course
>   With rocks and stones and trees![1]

Maintaining the alternating rhymed lines of the traditional ballad form, "A slumber . . ." both mimics and undermines the traditional dramatic development and *peripeteia* of its content. A perfect exercise in lyrical concision, the most estranging and among the most exquisite of the *Lyrical Ballads,* "A slumber . . ." seems to have the sole goal of constating the difference in state between a "thing" then and "now." It does this in two symmetrical stanzas, and the historical event or action that changed the one into the other stands between these as a blank, a descriptive and narrative void. There is, in short, no narrative representation of demise here, no object dropping off the "complex scene" of either dream-like or conscious life. But neither was any human coordination of complexity the subject of "A slumber . . ." to begin with: the speaker to whom "she seemed a thing" insensible to time while alive, "now" understands that misperception of constancy to belong to a past defined not by interaction but by his own "slumber." For "A slumber" is the unlikely, entitling subject of this poem, and "a

---

1. Butler and Green, p. 164: "A slumber . . .," ll. 1–8.

thing," its perceived object. Both subject and object are defined, *like poetry*, Wordsworth contends, by the interactions of which they are made. Yet, in "A slumber . . ." the poet "dares" to tell a story not of actions resulting in the perceived loss of an object, but of an objectification of inaction, the reification, or making-"thing," of a perceived object, "she." Any subject whose "spirit" has been "seal[ed]" off from perception can indeed only perceive any other as insensate "thing." Never having been a locus of the actions and interactions of which subjects, objects, and "the language really used by men" are composed, neither "she" nor the slumbering subject to whom "she" "seemed a thing" embodies even a temporary nexus of the "sensations and ideas" that, co-present in the course of experience, fail to coincide in Wordsworthian narratives at length.[2] No less than the life-enabling incapacity of what we call "life" to coincide with geometry,[3] that failure is not the fault of the narratives, but, rather, present evidence of what we might call their "lucidity."

2. Cf. Susan Eilenberg, *Strange Power of Speech. Wordsworth, Coleridge, and Literary Possession* (New York: Oxford University Press, 1992): "while Lucy was alive [the poet] had no need to think precisely about what she was. She was at once too ambiguous and too unambiguous: too changelessly herself to need a name, which implies the possibility of alteration or absence" (124). Building upon Eilenberg's astute observation of the "changeless" subject, "she," presented in "A slumber . . .," we can say that the challenge of change that instead compels us "to think precisely about what she," or any subject or object of perception, "was," arises whenever the "sensations and ideas" comprising our temporal experience cancel rather than supplement each other—a cognitive failure the "feeling" of which both Kant and Wordsworth name "sublime."

3. See Part I, Chap. 6, for detailed analyses of some of the geometrically delineable, scenographic narratives composed and undone by the speaker's actions in *The Prelude*, including the account of "hav[ing] hung [above] the raven's nest" "suspended" by the countervailing forces of gravity and "the blast that blew amain" (I: 330–339); the extensive episode of the stolen rowboat (I: 357–400); the description of the collapsing visual planes produced by "hang[ing] down-bending from the side of a slow-moving boat . . . on still water" (IV:256–276); the step-by-step depiction of accelerating acts of ice-skating able "to cut across" "the reflex of a star that . . . gleamed/Upon the glassy plain," as if drawing with "steel" a "line of motion" so "rapid" as to intersect that of light itself (I: 433–463). For Wordsworth's explicit consciousness of his own purposeful representational use and destruction of geometric form, articulated in a spare

The *absence* of activity that was the "thing" "she seem'd" in "A slumber . . ." is made present through a string of highly unconventional images compounded in each verse line. Beginning with the demotion of his own "spirit" to the grammatical status of an object "seal[ed]" by a "slumber" of indeterminate origin and length, the speaker of the poem compels its reader to wonder how and, moreover, when he could have perceived whatever "[s]he seem'd" to be. Similarly, the speaker's assertion that he possessed "no human fears," made strictly undefinable by the grammatical placement of its adjective (i.e., meaning *either* "fears" that, as a "human," he *doesn't* have, *or* "fears," that are not "human," that he *does*), suggests his own status as "human" subject is indeterminate, or, at very least, that, when it comes to "fears," there are, and he may possess, others of another, unknown kind. The experience of a "she" who "seemed" instead "a thing" seems to underscore within the speaker a pre-existing estrangement from the subject of experience we have assumed him, *as* speaker, to be, just as, conversely, his application of the modifier, "human," in a context in which, by all normative standards, it should be gratuitous, had already unsettled our understanding of the "human" in relation to himself. The equation of a person, "she," with "a thing" "that seemed" negatively capable of "not feel[ing]" makes its double incongruity—the predication of a human subject as inhuman object and that inhuman object as subject of no "earthly" action—disturbingly plain: "a thing" is as little a "she" as it, "a thing," can "feel," and the speaker's crossing back and forth between the poles of the chiastic exchange of human/nonhuman qualities he sets up ("*I* had *no human fears*"/ "a *thing* that could *not feel*") affords no identifiable subject or vehicle for narrative development or change. The final line of the opening stanza employs another apparently gratuitous or superfluous modifier to qualify a nearly lexically identical, rhyming noun: like "fears" specified to be "human," the alternative to "earthly years" is far from clear. Indeed, in attributing the power of "touch" to literally intangible "earthly years," Wordsworth, while appearing to resort to the device of personification he openly reviled, goes further than any literary device could take him to awaken fears rather than put them to sleep. Like the mortifying, entirely imaginary acts of Keats' "living hand . . . if it were dead," Wordsworth's "touch of earthly years," by compounding an

vocabulary remarkably similar to Dickinson's some decades later, see *The Prelude*, II: 203–205: "But who shall parcel out/his intellect by geometric rules,/ Split like a province into round and square."

ambiguity of qualification mirroring that of "human fears" with a new uncertainty regarding assigned grammatical roles (i.e., whether "touch" names an aspect of "earthly years" or "earthly years," an aspect of "touch"), comes as close to eliminating temporal difference in the "thing" to which it is negatively attributed ("that could not feel") as any "poetic" or prosaic use of the—inherently temporal—medium of language can effect.[4]

Complicating "things" further, "nothing"—to use the colloquial, spatial reification of negation—could "be further from" the imaginary exchanges of human and inhuman, and active and passive qualities compiled in stanza one than the state of thing-like, internal inertia described, after the break that is the center of the poem, in stanza two. Even the change signaled by the introduction of the present, "now," as the poem resumes, is not one the reader can refer to the "she" already said to have "seemed a thing" in stanza one. Described as never having "felt the touch of earthly years" personifying, from the imaginary perspective of a "thing," the temporality of existence itself,[5] "she" is described in stanza two as divested of all the interactive modes of experience to which, resembling "a thing," "she" was never subject in the

4. In *Wordsworth's Style. Figures and Themes in the Lyrical Ballads of 1800* (Lincoln: University of Nebraska Press, 1967), Roger N. Murray singles out this "personification" for commentary as one of the most "memorable" of "Wordsworth's metaphors," effectively taking Wordsworth's singular *opposition* of poetry to "Matters of Fact" full circle by attributing to the poet the capability to replace imaginative "comparisons" with the "described" "facts" of the "reality" of a "world" in which "real and ideal" are instead identical: "Something puts lines in our faces, to call it the *touch* of earthly years is to describe the indescribable, to fill in with high imagination the vacancy left by our abstractions. But high imagination—Wordsworth would in this case have insisted on calling it fancy— is not enough. For poetry to record and not simply imagine, it must do more than make comparisons: it must cause us to see that in reality all its comparisons are facts ... Wordsworth's vision was of a world where distinctions of abstract and concrete, animate and inanimate, and real and ideal remain only where the poet has not yet cast his glance, has not yet described things as they really are. In that world the touch of earthly years is fact, not fancy" (131–132).

5. A century and a half before Heidegger, "being in time" ("Dasein in der Zeit") was how Kant defined the particular being of human beings in general, in that our "internal" experience or subjecthood depends not only on each person's integral "relation" ("Beziehung") to that which is "outside" or "external to me"

first place, all the coordinations of "motion" with discrete perceptions that human subjectivity regularly enacts: "No motion has she now, no force;/She neither hears nor sees."[6] As if "representing" both that double absence of experience and the tomb-like "slumber" of his own "spirit," the actual advent of death is entirely elided in the spare juxtaposition of the poem's two stanzas by its speaker. Even as the underscoring of its division by distinct rhyme schemes (abab; cdcd) and tenses (preterite; present) creates a powerful anticipation of narrated change, the poem's pointed omission of the event distinguishing "now" from a temporally ambiguous prior state suggests that, in the case of this previously seeming "thing," any real demarcation between past and present is either irrelevant or unutterable, inappropriate or unavailable to the objectification and reflection of its enactment in "real language."[7] The "she" who, as described in stanza one, "seemed a thing that could not feel" an already estranged sense of time before, is described in stanza two as bereft of the bases of all "feel[ing]" "now," and, rather than "seem[ing]" insensible to a purely figurative "touch of earthly years," as unable to sense the material stuff of which the actual earth is made. The speaker's formerly "slumber[ing]" "spirit" finds itself awoken too late, capable only of recognizing a previous capacity for "motion" and "force"

("ausser mir ist"), but on our ability to perceive, by way of that relation, both the otherwise imperceptible fact of temporal "change" ("Veränderung"), and, reciprocally, "that I myself exist determined in time" (dass ich selbst in der Zeit bestimmt existiere"); see Kant, *KrV* B XL-XLI, III: 38–39.

6. Butler and Green, "A slumber. . .," ll.5–6.

7. The blank space of representation in the middle of "A slumber . . ." both supports and negates Jones' claim that Paul de Man got it wrong when, in his well-known discussion of the poem in "The Rhetoric of Temporality," he distinguished the real, non-successive "temporality of experience" from the "differential structure and constitutive function of all language" evidenced in the poem. While that early essay by de Man contains several critical misrepresentations which he himself later lamented, it would be more accurate to describe its attribution to the poem of an allegorical structure and consciousness as both supported by that blank (which is to say, what the poem is pointedly missing), in that no conscious perception or experience of death is *represented* in the poem, *and* negated by it, because no conscious experience or perception of death is *narrated* in the poem (representation and narration being the twin foundations of allegory, whether of acts of consciousness or of pure fiction). See Jones, *The 'Lucy Poems,'* pp. 210–211.

"now" that it has been superseded and "she" is fixed instead in the force of the earth's sway, an ongoing, unpunctuated motion itself as exempt from death as from change: "Roll'd round in earth's diurnal course/With rocks and stones and trees!"[8]

If there is a single more estranging line in Wordsworth's poetry—indeed in any poetic *corpus*—one would be hard pressed to find it.[9] For it is one thing to be a living body imagined "dead" by a speaker whose movement upon the earth toward it is interrupted by a sudden, "wayward thought," that is, to be whatever it is to be "Lucy" in "Strange fits," or, for that matter, to be a dead body known to be buried in a graveyard, the kind of earthly demarcated disappearance from the visible "scene" of action with which, most memorably, the interrupted story of the Boy of Winander elegiacally concludes, as the narrator recalls himself repeatedly "looking at the grave in which he lies."[10] But it is another thing entirely to be represented, from an impossibly extra-terrestrial and extra-temporal perspective, as an inert object caught within the regular "diurnal course" of the earth itself. Stranger still is the representation of the company this once "seem[ing]," "now" in fact reified, wholly insensible "thing" keeps. For, more alien to life on earth than ceasing to "feel" an uncannily personified "touch of earthly years" is to not feel *and* be "roll'd round" in a kind of metonymic contagion

---

8. Butler and Green, "A slumber...," ll.7–8.

9. One can only wonder at the not uncommon critical assertion that being "roll'd round" with pieces of earth is a good, indeed, a splendid thing. For exemplary descriptions of the "transcendent peace of spirit" and "transcendent calm" Wordsworth is said to achieve in the closing lines of "A slumber...," as he "divin[es] the eternal in his relationship with his beloved" and "celebrate[s] life," see Marchant, *Principles ...*, pp. 48, 33. Certainly, even the view of Wordsworth as happy pantheist must detect the final exclamation of horror ("!") with which he describes the prospect of a "now" inanimate human body he had believed insensible to time, jumbled indiscriminately with outcroppings of organic and petrified matter by the perpetual motion of centrifugal force itself.

10. *The Prelude*, V: 396–399: "And through that churchyard when my way has led/On summer evenings I believe that there/A long half-hour together I have stood/Mute—looking at the grave in which he lies!" ["And there along that bank, when I have passed/At evening, I believe that oftentimes/A full half-hour together I have stood/Mute, looking at the grave in which he lies." (V: 419–422, 1805)]

"with rocks and stones and trees!" Each of the things Wordsworth
names in this short paratactic list throws our sense of the next, both as
word and as object, out of synch, even as all remain held together, within
this grammatically, syntactically, and syllabically simplest of verse lines,
by the purely associative force of, in Husserl's words, the infinitely useful,
illogical "little word, 'and.'"[11]

For, it is the nature of "earthly" "trees" to live like living bridges
between the earth and the sun, their continuing extension in opposite
directions generated as much by roots moving away from the sun
as by branches moving toward it, the same dual orientation used
to figure our own lives' extension between the invisible depths of
experience and memory and actual unfolding of actions and events.
The "trees" of "A slumber . . . ," by contrast, appear either permanently
uprooted or impossibly perpetually inverted, "growing" downside
up, in the "course" of the poet's line. Juxtaposed with inanimate
objects indifferently gathered within a single centrifugal field, these
most expansive, living and life-giving embodiments of the earth
appear instead indistinguishable, in all but name, from the terrestrial
ruins or remains of life called "rocks and stones." Yet still more
disturbing is the cognitive effect, of the very kind Wordsworth
describes in his "Note to 'The Thorn,'" enacted by the poet's

---

11. Husserl makes this linguistic observation when writing of the *a priori*
sense of interrelated "'pluralities'" (citing British mathematician, logician, and
economist William Stanley Jevons), "groupings" ("Mengen"), "collective relation"
("kollektive Verbindung"), "collection altogether" ("Gesamtkollektion"), "acts
that go together" ("Zusammenhängende Akte"), and "acts of collecting"
("kollegierende Akte") exhibited by our unthinking reliance upon the universally
useful, thoroughly irrational "Wörtchen, *und*" ("little word, *and*") not only in
common discourse but the logical disciplines of number, arithmetic and
mathematics. See Edmund Husserl, *Philosophie der Arithmetik* (1890-1901),
Husserliana, Bd. 12, Hrgb. Lothar Eley (Berlin: Springer, 1972), XII: 62-63,
74.10-11; 75.1-2; 75.8-9, 21; 75.10; 75.31-15; 75.35-36. *et passim.* I have
analyzed Husserl's mathematical and philosophical investigations of the purely
differential, collective and contextual relations and associations constitutive, on
his view, of all modes of cognition in "'A now not *toto caelo* a not now:' Husserl
and the 'Origin' of Difference, from Number to Literature," *Phenomenology to
the Letter. Husserl and Literature,* ed. Philippe Haensler and Rochelle Tobias
(Berlin: de Gruyter, 2020), pp. 1-31.

inclusion, within this minimalist polysyndeton, of redundant "rocks" and "stones."[12]

For no physical, quantifiable, contextual, or practical criterion distinguishes the objects to which "rocks and stones" refer. The only hard and fast distinction between *these* inanimate things is the purely nominal one of their names. In tandem with the "now" inert subject, or "she," of Wordsworth's poem, this short inventory of objects unrolls or unravels into a series of questions for the reader that, like the things it designates, occur in no particular order, and prove as recalcitrant to conception as an arbitrary assemblage of "rocks and stones." First, and most conspicuously: why would the poet choose to include in so brief a list two synonyms for a single signified? Are "rocks and stones," *like* the non-identical sounds of the two etymologically distinct words that name them, really different in a way we cannot define but that the language we use, operating independently of its comprehension, indicates? Or do "rocks and stones" signify a purely verbal distinction without a difference, but for that of their habitual use? And, if so, why indeed use them *together*, if not to signify that words themselves, in stark contrast to their interchangeable sense, may be as thing-like and rigid as the objects they designate? Do "rocks and stones," in other words, resemble rocks and stones—not as verbal referents may be mystically believed to resemble objects but as "things" similarly differing only in their formation in time? Finally, if categorical distinctions, like that between persons ("she") and things ("rocks and stones and trees"), and qualitative distinctions among different things, such as "rocks and stones" and "trees," and purely nominal distinctions between non-distinct things, like "rocks and stones," are all either attenuated or obliterated in being "roll'd round" "with" each other, then is the "earth" in whose "diurnal course" all these inalterably revolve, the same earth as we know and experience it—ground and basis of "earthly years" and "human fears"—or, rather, a deathless jumble of "thing[s]" and words, and words as things, that, relieved of all attachment to action or idea, are merely carried by the "course" of a power in which they take no "active" "part"?

For on such an earth the difference between inanimate and living— between being "stone" and being "tree"—has no meaning; and the difference between "rocks and stones," that has no meaning in life,

---

12. See Chap. 2, n.4, this study. The minimal number of elements whose association by a single repeated conjunction qualifies their sequencing as a polysyndeton is three.

appears meaningful only because no life, but solely indiscriminate motion, associates them. Whereas in "Strange passions . . .," the sudden, apparent "drop[ping"] of the "moon" "behind" the desired object to which a "dear" "path" led, prompted in its place "wayward thoughts" of death, the "she" whose death is neither suggested nor represented by any empirical occurrence in "A slumber . . ." remains forever inextricable from an unending force of motion no one can initiate, let alone see. For it is specifically *not* the downward and inward thrust of gravity that both allows us to move at will and grounds and positions us and the objects we perceive, but rather the mechanical thrust away from the center of a circular motion working *against* gravity that holds this "she" dispossessed of life and internal force to an earth whose own "diurnal course" no one living on earth can perceive. In the course of this radically abbreviated ballad, whose two rhyming quatrains of alternating eight- and six-beat lines present the blank space separating and negating any narrative relation between them as unfathomable, the "thing" "she" "seemed" is "now" become one senseless thing among many. If ever there were poetry more prosaic, like the change from life to death that the poem deletes, one would not know it; and if ever there were prose more poetic, more demonstrative of the "interest which the mind attaches to words, not only as symbols of the passions, but as *things*, active and efficient, which are themselves part of the passion," we could not read it, for this would be prose without even a blank space intervening to indicate experience lost forever to the mind, the prose of a spirit that cannot know if it slumbers or wakes: a spirit "seal[ed]," then as "now," from the very language purposed to represent it.[13] In its ability to disabuse us of confusing language with either practically dispensable "symbols"[14] *or* the purely material stuff of rocks and stones and trees, there may be no language more "real," which is to say, more potent than the bare words with which the poet awakens his reader's "spirit" from "slumber"—except, perhaps, for those describing the unparalleled "power" of "Imagination" to which this study turns next.

13. Ibid.
14. Ibid.

Chapter 9

"Imagination"

Precisely the comparative differences by which we orient our actions on earth[1]—between up and down, person and "thing," subjects and objects, reference and referent—are paramount to the literal "passages" in *The Prelude* that any analysis of Wordsworth's poetics of "the language really used by men" must consider: the naming and representation of the ("so-called") "Power" of "Imagination" that eclipse the narrator's account of his physical traversal of the Alps, along with their apparently unrelated narrative sequel, in the so-called "Gondo Gorge" passage, in Bk. VI. An anti-climax unsurpassed by any in English poetry before or since, Wordsworth's narrative of his and his walking companions' failure to reach the goal of their long journey on foot, or, rather, their success in reaching and indeed going beyond that goal—the actual crossing of Simplon Pass—*while failing to perceive that they had done so*, gives way to the most climactic near-apostrophe in Wordsworth's or any Romantic poet's work. Just as the forward motion of their journey is provided not by the mesmerizing hoofbeats or gliding "steel" of a second vehicular body, to which their own bodies, moving along known "paths," are adjoined, but by the travelers' own unprecedented steps, the particular focus upon which they "fix" their attention is also no external, celestial body but the idea of a visible highpoint they carry inside them: the geographical turning point of the mountains and projected summit of their own purposeful progress that they aspire, through steadfast mounting motion, at once to attain and to see.

Unguided and ignorant of the path they must take to reach that goal, the travelers discover they have been misdirected by their "hopes."

1. Cf. Kant's practical demonstration of the intellectual instantiation of difference, and prophetic demystification of all attempts to define and locate "left" and "right" "orientations" empirically, the great essay, "What does orienting oneself in thinking mean?" ("Was heisst sich im Denken orientieren?" in Kant, *Schriften zur Metaphysik und Logik I*, V: 267–283.

While "the only track now visible" appeared to offer the travelers "conspicuous invitation to ascend/A lofty mountain," that visible upward trajectory—unlike the "climb" to "Lucy"'s cottage—proves to have been mis-taken to begin with. For the travelers have in fact already passed the point of passage at which they aimed, and the path they must take to retrace their steps leads, in every sense, not up but down. Wordsworth narrates:

> Hastily rose our Guide,
> Leaving us at the Board; a while we lingered,
> Then paced the beaten downward way that led
> Right to a rough stream's edge and there broke off,
>   The only track now visible was one
> That from the torrent's further brink held forth
> Conspicuous invitation to ascend
> A lofty mountain. After brief delay
> Crossing the unbridged stream, that road we took
> And clomb with eagerness, till anxious fears
> Intruded, for we failed to overtake
> Our comrades gone before. By fortunate chance,
> While every moment added doubt to doubt,
> A Peasant met us, from whose mouth we learned
> That to the Spot which had perplexed us first
> We must descend, and there should find the road,
> Which in the stony channel of the Stream
> Lay a few steps, and then along its banks;
> And, that our future course, all plain to sight,
> Was downwards, with the current of that stream.[2]

The reversal of their "course, all plain to sight," from onwards and upwards to "downwards" and backwards, redirects the travelers' steps toward a "future" already situated in a past whose significance they had not recognized at the time: a "Spot" whose formerly "perplex[ing]" sense is now revealed to them as critical to their progress. Given conflicting external indications, the travelers' misstep and unknowing overshooting of the very goal at which their journey aimed must instead be redressed by specifically non-spatial means. It is not what they see before them,

---

2. *The Prelude* VI: 566–581. The 1805 version (V: 500–519) is considerably more periphrastic up to its nearly identical, final nine lines.

as "every moment added doubt to doubt," but the "word[s]" which "[c]ame in reply" to their repeated "question[ing]"—entirely prosaic words endowed with independent, nearly physical status, not only by their uncharacteristic citation in italics, but by the bluntly empirical report of their issuance from a fully depersonalized, anonymous source ("every word that from the Peasant's lips/Came in reply")—that convey the violent sense of incommensurability which imposes itself upon the travelers now, and the depth of shock arising within them from their encounter with an external *utterance* rather than scenographic object, mirrors the sudden dropping, not of the moon or any other natural body, but of their own inner, upwardly oriented "hopes":

> Loth to believe what we so grieved to hear,
> For still we had hopes that pointed to the clouds,
> We questioned him again, and yet again;
> But every word that from the Peasant's lips
> Came in reply, translated by our feelings,
> Ended in this, *that we had crossed the Alps.*[3]

"Translated" or carried across by "our feelings," just as the travelers' feet had carried them, unknowing, across the Alps, the selfsame words the travelers encounter remain impervious to attempts to affect their consequence by displacing their "materially different," "prosaic" sense through emotively projected "translat[ion]." In a manner particularly revelatory of the inconsequence of translation to critical encounters of any kind, the historically recurrent, self-compounding inflation of subjective projection that is part and parcel of the peddling of every (necessarily) advertised "globalism," from the monetized to the sacred, and the replacement through displacement of concrete philological objects by the tertiary objects of "translation studies" that facilitate all these,[4] as if subjectively substituted translations were themselves objects rather than evasions of the resistance to erasure of words themselves,

---

3. *The Prelude,* VI: 586–591 (emphasis in text).

4. Cf. Benjamin, "The Task of the Translator," ("Die Aufgabe des Übersetzers," *Illuminationen,* Hrsg. Sigfried Unseld (Frankfurt: Suhrkamp, 1977), P. 51, 56: "That a translation, no matter how good it is said to be, can never be of any significance for the original, is clear" ("Dass eine Übersetzung niemals, so gut sie auch sei, etwas für das Original zu bedeuten vermag, leuchtet ein"); "the relation between content and language is entirely different in the original and

is perhaps nowhere better deflated than by Wordsworth here, as "repeated" attempts to will words away, to transpose or "translate" them by personal "feelings," "[e]nd" instead in their emphatic repetition, "[e]nded in this, *that we had crossed the Alps.*" And what then arises *in the poem*, in the place of the diversion from an unbridgeable breach between experience and expectation attempted by its displacing "translat[ion]"—by misdirections of any kind—is the single, unrelated word, "Imagination." In the lost travelers' insuperable encounter with the unchanging "words" of the "Peasant," Wordsworth represents the dynamic of interrupted experience narrated mimetically in the Lucy poems "literally," i.e., as a lived encounter *with* "the real language of men," the language of actual action and interaction, itself. A poetic representation of the central tenet of Wordsworth's poetic theory, and one of the supreme summits, and most powerful reversals of expectations, composed in English poetry, the passage describes the active force or "Power" experienced by the traveler–poet when "real language," in contradistinction to both empirical givens and subjective

translation … the language of translation … remains thereby incommensurate, violent and foreign to its own content. This brokenness impedes all further translation" ("das Verhältnis des Gehalts zur Sprache völlig verschieden ist im Original und Übersetzung … die Sprache der Übersetzung … bleibt dadurch ihrem eigenen Gehalt gegenüber unangemessen, gewaltig und fremd. Diese Gebrochenheit verhindert jede Übertragung"). The sole interest of Benjamin in translation, that of the "mode of meaning" or "intending" ("Art des Meinens" [55, 58]) informing all language, or what he calls "pure language" ("die reine Sprache"), which the "brokenness" or second-hand relation of all translations to content is especially apt to reveal, is as opposed as any view of language can be to the subjectively projected conception of "translation studies" as an object in itself. While translations are, for Benjamin, themselves the deadest of "dead" ends, and any "translation theory" ("Theorie der Übersetzung") that, "mistaking occasion for essence" ("heisse … Grund und Wesen … verwechseln"), bases itself in "the subjectivity of those who come later rather than the life proper to language and its works" ("die Subjektivität der Nachgebornen statt im eigenen Leben der Sprache und ihrer Werke") is "dead" ("tote" [54]) from its inception, his understanding of the purposeful "task" or "challenge" ("Aufgabe") of revealing in "works" "of language" how all languages work may come closest to Wordsworth's understanding of what poets do in writing in "real language," their purposeful exposure of the "life" of language, or "language really used by men."

aspirations, *acts upon him*, followed, without mediating explanation or mimetic narration, by a delayed "acknowledgement" of that confounding "Power" "now":

> Imagination—here the Power so called
> Through sad incompetence of human speech—
> That awful Power rose from the Mind's abyss
> Like an unfathered vapour that enwraps
> At once some lonely Traveller. I was lost,
> Halted without an effort to break through;
> But to my conscious soul I now can say,
> "I recognize thy glory"; in such strength
> Of usurpation, when the light of sense
> Goes out, but with a flash that has revealed
> The invisible world, doth Greatness make abode . . .[5]

In "Strange fits of passion" the exclamation of the traveler's sudden, visually induced fear are words he speaks to himself; in "A slumber . . .," a human "thing" is eulogized and words, brought to life by their equalization with the things they name. At the turning point of *The Prelude,* words are instead the origin of experience and that origin must come from outside the subject. They neither take the place of objects that, in disappearing, "slide" into the "mind" as "thoughts," nor "roll round" alongside an unearthly "thing" whose removal from the purview of a previously "slumber[ing]" mind can only be represented by blank space. Here language instead acts upon the mind in the pronounced *absence* of visible interaction with the world: the "objects" it names do not "immediately excite ... sympathies" but, on the contrary, have already, immediately, been missed.[6] It is not an imagined death, nor the

---

5. *The Prelude,* VI: 567–603. I have chosen to cite the 1850 version of this passage both for its own superior power of expression—the poet's heightening of descriptive tension through the addition of contrasting conjunctions ("But ... But ... but .." [VI: 590, 599, 602], his deletion of hackneyed "poetic diction" in the lines devoted to "Imagination" (cf. 1805 version: "here that Power/In the might of its endowments, came/Athwart me ... And now recovering in my Soul I say ..." [VI: 527–31]), and more forceful syntactic exposition overall—and because the description of "Imagination" in the 1850 text directly reflects that given in the "Essay, Supplementary to the Preface," discussed below.

6. See Chap. 2, n. 1, this study.

imagining of death, but "Imagination" that is a kind of death in this crucial passage, the loss of the self in the "lost" purpose of a self "[h]alted without an effort to break through." Writing as theorist of poetics, Wordsworth stipulates that "what . . . the Poet [does]," in "consider[ing] man" and the "objects that surround him as acting and re-acting upon each other," and composing "powerful descriptions" of such interactions in "real language" "arising out of repeated experience," are acts that must be carried forward by something unrelated to either active subjects or objects, the "co-presence of something regular." Yet, in the sudden encounter with another's "words," "Imagination," arising alone and unprecedented "from the Mind's abyss," does something most irregular to the self the poet represents, cutting him off equally from all communication with objects and words. For "here," in the absence of experience, the only "so-called" subject or agent of action *is* "Imagination": an action allowing for no human interaction and a subject standing outside the human ken of language. Like the travelers' passionate misreading of nature, "human speech" itself, the poet laments, misspeaks in saying "Imagination." "Imagination—here the Power so called/Through sad incompetence of human speech—" may well be said to be "'recognize[d]'" in *its* "'glory'; in such strength/Of usurpation, when the light of sense/Goes out," by an "'I'" speaking in a citational present "to" a "soul" "now" called "conscious." But Wordsworth writes "'*thy* glory,'" and the subject of that second-person possessive, and object of the statement of recognition this cited "'I'" performs, is *not* "Imagination," as the climactic structure of the passage implies, but rather, and at an undefined temporal remove from that climax, "my conscious soul." "Imagination," the usurper of sense that severs "the Mind" from external *and* internal images, cannot even be, in "human speech," a proper object of apostrophe: in order to be imaged as some thing or power available to recognition and address, "Imagination" must first be confounded, grammatically and temporally, with exactly what it was not then and is not "now," consciousness itself.[7]

7. The landmark discussion of the passage by Geoffrey Hartman, in *Wordsworth's Poetry: 1787–1814* (New Haven: Yale University Press, 1975 [1964]), extends that confusion to the canon of its reception by acknowledging and defining "his 'conscious soul'" to be the clear grammatical object of the poet's address while nonetheless identifying the entire passage as an "apostrophe to Imagination" (p. 41). The fact that Wordsworth's "'I'" repeatedly blocks the direct relation of first to second person constituted in apostrophic address— first, by following an apparently apostrophic exclamation with a description of

Given the sublime experience of "Imagination" narrated in Bk. VI, it may come as a surprise to Wordsworth's reader that, whether in the traditional, "transcendental," or, as the poet here qualifies it, "so-called" sense, "Imagination" plays no meaningful part in the poetic interactions elaborated in the "Preface." It appears in the 1805 edition of the "Preface" as a supplemental "coloring" agent layered upon the "language really used by men": "The principal object, then, proposed in these poems was to choose incidents and situations from common life, and to relate or describe them—in as far as was possible in a selection of language really used by men—and at the same time, to throw over them a certain colouring of imagination."[8] Yet the 1805 "Preface" also identifies imaginative "colouring" with the conventional pejorative meaning of falsification, describing "deviat[ions]" from "real language" as rhetorical "colours"; and in the "Essay Supplementary to the Preface," "imagination" is said to characterize the perceived divergence of the *Lyrical Ballads* from the public view of poetry.[9] From the 1800 to 1815 edition of the "Preface," Wordsworth satirizes "critics" who "imagine that they have made a notable discovery" in pronouncing and denouncing deviations from poetic diction as "prosaisms." He treats the act of imagining as synonymous with conventional "first" impressions, arguing that "the language really spoken by men" can "form a distinction far greater than would at first be imagined"; and, in the Appendix to the "Preface," "the Reader" used to "extravagant and absurd diction" is derided for "imagin[ing] that he is *balked* of a particular enjoyment" in its absence.[10] Finally, the singular characterization of "Imagination" as an inevitable misnomer in the 1850 *Prelude* reframes an earlier, decidedly non-sublime expression of the same in the theory of the poetic nature of

its object in the third person: "Imagination!—here the Power so-called/ . . .that awful Power"; then, in directing the only second-person address that does occur in the passage not "to" "Imagination" but the consciousness that has since replaced it; and, ultimately, in distancing that consciousness entirely from the event by inserting self-mirroring quotation marks around its acknowledgment— "But to my conscious soul I now can say/'I recognize thy glory'"—may be read instead as prime demonstration of the apposite observation sandwiched between all these, i.e., "the sad incompetence of human speech" when its subject is "Imagination."

8. Owen and Smyser, I: 123.
9. Owen and Smyser, I: 142, 145, III: 80.
10. Owen and Smyser, I: 132, I: 133; I: 137, I: 162 (emphasis in text).

"real language" poetics pursued by Wordsworth in the "Essay Supplementary": "Poverty of language is the primary cause of the use which we make of the word, Imagination."[11]

The relative paucity of references to imagination in Wordsworth's major texts on poetics, and near erasure by a theory of prosaic "complex[ity]" sustained by "something" continuous and "regular," makes its retrospective referencing as "that awful Power," at the poetic climax of Wordsworth's narrative epic, appear less comprehensible still. Incomprehensible, yet perhaps consistently so, for the "Power" named "Imagination" in Bk VI of *The Prelude* is not "poetic," in Wordsworth's interactively "complex" sense, and the "knowledge" that may well be considered its "effect" is not knowledge in any traditional "philosophical" *or* poetical sense. It is rather knowledge that, as unbidden as the Peasant's uncolorful prose, directly contradicts all the travelers had imagined and are apt to imagine again. Wordsworth's theory of poetry equates poetry with prose and either references imagination slightingly, or states, or demonstrates, the inability of language to reference it properly. The "Imagination" named by the prosaically enlightened traveler is a "Power" to destroy poetry: while originating in the mind's interaction with "the language really used by men"—"But every word that from the Peasant's lips/Came in reply, translated by our feelings,/Ended in this, *that we had crossed the Alps*"—the "knowledge" that interaction "effect[s]" does not, per the "Essay Supplementary," follow *from* but rather is *of* a "power" that puts all "knowledge" at risk. Embodying "the true difficulty" indicated in Wordsworth's theory of poetry, it also disables the interactive basis of poetry and its effects. For "Imagination" here names the mind interacting with the world and with words in such a way that the two interactions, separate in object and in time, are not diachronically related to each other— by either "reflection," the "representati[on]" of "feelings" in "thoughts," the "produc[tion] of habits of mind," or the "mechanical" repetition of "something regular"—but, instead, immediately *intersect*, the latter linguistic encounter eradicating the former encounter with phenomena and thus truly *acting* as poetry in the "end."

In stark contrast to the disabling contradiction of expectation by geography first articulated by an unknown peasant's "mouth" and reiterated by the narrator "word" for word, the "awful Power," thwarting all further physical *and* narrative progress, that that contradiction generates is displaced by the poet onto an entirely nonexperiential,

11. Owen and Smyser, III: 81.

"invisible world" in which no thing but a personified "Greatness make[s] abode." The conspicuously exotic comparison between a "now" "conscious soul" whose "'glory'" can only be "'recognize[d]'" in retrospect and a timeless archetypal geography ("like the mighty flood of Nile/Poured from his fount of Abyssinian clouds/To fertilise the whole Egyptian plain"[12]) introduced, after the fact, to populate that "invisible world" figuratively, replacing and *in place of* "the language really used by men," exemplify precisely the ornate "poetic diction" Wordsworth's poetics and poetry reject, the stock impediments to any active, poetic attempt to "discover what is really important to men."[13] Such fanciful rewriting of "Imagination" in nonexperiential, "metaphysical" imagery reappears sporadically throughout the unsteady course of experience narrated in *The Prelude*. When, in a nearly parodic replay and inversion of the awful extinction of "the light of sense" at Simplon Pass in Book VI, the poet describes the second-hand "light" of "the Moon" successfully glimpsed on Mount Snowdon in Book XIV, he proceeds to re-"name" "Imagination" by redefining it as instead synonymous with what it is not, "exalted" "reason." As if cleaning his slate of all already recorded loss, he replaces its profoundly disruptive "Power" with a new-found assumption of "truth": "Imagination, which in truth/Is but another name for absolute power/And clearest insight, amplitude of mind/And reason, in her most exalted mood".[14] One might

12. *The Prelude*, VI: 602–616.

13. Owen and Smyser, II: 456.

14. *The Prelude*, XIV: 189–192. In his "Conclusion: Imagination" to *Wordsworth's Philosophic Song* (Cambridge: Cambridge University Press, 2007), Simon Jarvis accurately describes the "further diffusion of the term's meaning" effected by this definition of "Imagination" in Bk XIV, suggesting in addition that, "[w]herever he tries to say in verse what imagination is, Wordsworth becomes more than usually cataloguing or paratactic." Surprisingly, Jarvis makes no mention of the naming of Imagination in Bk VI for which Wordsworth is, rightly, most famed, and which, while not offered in the form of a "cataloguing" definition in verse, is as active, dramatic and non-"paratactic" a statement as any Wordsworth's poetry contains. Similarly, Jarvis's own substitutional definition of "imagination," as an indiscriminate "capacity for experience" (also, "attention to experience"), is difficult to reconcile with the paralyzing loss of all access to experience that Wordsworth unequivocally attributes to the "awful Power" of "Imagination" in Bk. VI, itself just as acutely divorced from the mystifying experience of "ideology" and "idolatry" that Jarvis instead describes (pp. 222, 220, 215, 35–83).

conclude that, by the close of *The Prelude*, the poet, having learned to write over the radically disorienting experience of "that awful Power" with a latter-day "amplitude" of "reason," has earned the right to adopt it as the retrospective "theme" of the preceding poem,[15] recuperating "Imagination" as the recognizable (if stubbornly singly unidentifiable) standard-bearer of poetry overall, rather than unforeseeable "halt[ing]" of his own poem. Yet, in positioning itself above experience, on a par with "angels" cartoonishly depicted as "stopped upon the wing by sound/Of harmony from heaven's remotest spheres,"[16] that thematic revision leaves the interactive vision of the world and words of prose behind, and with them, one can argue more generally, Wordsworth's theory of poetry as well.[17]

For if "Imagination," "so-called" at an impassable crossroad of cross-purposes, improperly names a "Power" from which no "knowledge" can be had, and if *"there"*—in the transit effected between power and *knowledge*, rather than magical "harmony" of "spheres" "remotest" of all from the Peasant's plain speech—"is where the true difficulty lies" still, it is perhaps somewhere else in *The Prelude*, unidentified, and so effectively "buried" in plain sight, that "Imagination," instead of necessarily misnamed, is made into a form of knowledge instead. For, once the narrator's retrospective flight of fancy, from an experience of immediate, mental and perceptual exile into a mythically bountiful Egypt, ends, the

15. *The Prelude*, XIV: 206–207.

16. *The Prelude*, XIV: 98–99.

17. Hartman helpfully points out that the nearly contemporaneous composition of the Snowden and Simplon Pass sections, in February through March and April 1804 respectively, both marks them as "two rival highpoints of *The Prelude*" and "confirms Wordsworth's tendency to avoid an apocalyptic self-consciousness" (*Wordsworth's Poetry* ..., p. 63). While their structural positioning at the end and near midpoint of the poem would indeed confirm such an observation—the intellectualized redefinition of "that awful Power" appearing at "remotest" remove of nearly three thousand verse lines—the fact that Wordsworth's arresting designation of a misnamed "Power" of "Imagination" within the first-person narrative context of Bk. VI was in fact composed *after* its non-narrative domestication in Bk XIV, as "but another name for reason" and "angels" of the sort Milton had actively blown from the "heavens" several "poetic" generations ago, must confound all chronologically based appeals to either psychological maturation or ideological motivation in attempts to account for what Wordsworth does with and to Imagination in this first great English-language epic to follow, in several senses of the term, Milton's.

poem and the travelers continue along their earth-bound way, "[a]nd, with the half-shaped road, which we had missed,/Entered a narrow chasm."[18] The absolute absence of any transition between the narrator's relation of the travelers' resumption of their journey and the explosive passage, written entirely in the third person, that immediately succeeds it—no mention of internal "hopes" or "aspirations" here, nor even of any act of seeing, to intercede between them—repeats, in an apparently descriptive or mimetic mode, the force of his blinding encounter with "Imagination." Yet this description, if it is one, seems to come, so to speak, from nowhere, describing no place that persons can perceive, no encounter on the part of any subject with either objects or words, and, along with feelings, leaves all mention of "Imagination" out of the picture:

> ... The brook and road
> Were fellow-travellers in this gloomy Strait,
> And with them did we journey several hours
> At a slow pace. The immeasurable height
> Of woods decaying, never to be decayed,
> The stationary blasts of waterfall,
> And in the narrow rent at every turn
> Winds thwarting winds, bewildered and forlorn,
> The torrents shooting from the clear blue sky,
> The rocks that muttered close upon our ears,
> Black drizzling crags that spoke by the way-side
> As if a voice were in them, the sick sight
> And giddy prospect of the raving stream,
> The unfettered clouds, and region of the Heavens,
> Tumult and peace, the darkness and the light,
> Were all like workings of one mind ...[19]

Whatever the "workings of one mind" may look "like," there has never been nor will there ever be a "chasm," or any topographable form, in which these qualities are contained.[20] The replacement of visual detail

18. *The Prelude*, VI: 621–622.

19. *The Prelude.*, VI: 622– 637.

20. Cf. Marchant's pertinent observation that the descent into the "chasm," which he identifies with the Simplon Pass, represents the poet's "[a]pprehension of the great non-human universe": "[The poet] perceives the unknown, and (in any way he yet knows) unknowable. The poem then is the appropriate 'knowing'" (*Principles . . .*, p. 29).

by the series of gerundive verbs representing the "sick sight" and "giddy prospect" of this thoroughly dynamic "scene" recall the disturbance of the perceptible stability of nature provoked by the poet's many forays into nature as a boy in Bk I: his hanging "above the raven's nest . . . almost (or so it seemed)/Suspended by the blast that blew amain" (I: 331–334); rowing with his "view" "fixed" "upon the summit of a craggy ridge," when "from behind that craggy steep, till then/The horizon's bound, a huge peak, black and huge,/as if with voluntary power instinct,/ Upreared its head . . . and still,/For so it seemed, with purpose of its own/And measured motion, like a living thing/Strode after me" (I: 369– 385); wheeling back on skates so that his "rapid motion" "Stopped short; yet still the solitary cliffs/Wheeled by me—even as if the earth had rolled/With visible motion her diurnal round!" (I: 458–460); and the Boy of Winander hanging suspended in "a gentle shock of mild surprise," when the "concourse wild" of "mimic hootings" from owls "responsive to his call" is broken by a silence obliterating mimicry and response alike (V: 375–386). Resulting in an experience of experience increasingly divided and ultimately unhinged, these mutually echoing, individual narratives of willful actions and the apparently autonomous "motion" they unleash, engrave themselves in the reader's memory with their own forceful precision. In so doing, they appear in retrospect to rehearse or "set the stage" for the unstage-able, so-called "Gondo Gorge" passage just quoted.

"Still" (to employ the poet's ambiguous modifier of choice), no precipitating action is narrated to provoke, and nothing can prepare its reader for what this particular passage describes. Following the arresting encounter with the Peasant's words, sudden, seeming apostrophe of "Imagination," and resumption of their "journey," onward and "downward" as directed, "for several hours at a slow pace," the abrupt appearance of this unending, upended universe in verse is mediated for the reader by no narrating voice and excludes all mention of the travelers themselves. Arising as their and the poem's "regular" progress proceeds, the irreducibly "complex scene," exchanging down for up, and speech for inarticulate sound, intervenes in the narrative mid-iambic pentameter line (VI: 625) after a full-stop enjambment and long-vowel spondee. Shorn of any prefatory explanation and squarely separated metrically from the narrated events that precede it, the unsee-able, distinctly non-geometrical "chasm" the passage describes exceeds the very parameters of mimetic imaging by combining stasis and motion in representations of objects themselves only available to perception in either a static or dynamic state ("woods," "waterfall," "wind"). In short, while sayable, the "scene" represented in this description is, strictly speaking, unperceivable, which is to say, untraceable to any seat of perception not by omission but of necessity. The phenomenal enclosure briefly referenced as "narrow" before the passage begins may well "stand" for the unsettling "depth" of experience at which the repeated crossings of perceived natural boundaries narrated in *The Prelude* aim: that of a "Power" "thwarting" comprehension whose stated "'recogni[tion]'" must actively displace so as to replace it, and which "human speech," indeed "incompeten[t]" to name properly, misnames for the very capacity to image visually that it usurps in the first place, "Imagination."

Arising in the midst of "something regular," the "mechanical" act of proceeding, step after step, past the verbal crossroads at which his senses failed him and "that awful Power rose from the Mind's abyss," the so-called "Gondo Gorge" passage "descends," so to speak, into that abyss, representing what no one could possibly see in perhaps the single most powerful of all of Wordsworth's descriptions.[21] Prosaic while irreducibly

21. Along with the uneventful, steady descent on foot it describes in direct contrast to the stories of youthful daring written at the same time, the early date of composition of this passage, contemporaneous with both the Lucy Poems (1799) and first two Books of *The Prelude,* and nearly contemporaneous with the original publication of the "Preface" (*Lyrical Ballads,* 2nd ed. [1800]), sets it chronologically apart from the later versions of "Imagination" typically viewed, in Hartman's words, as the poem's "rival highpoints." The singular, contextually and historically independent effect of this passage heading from nowhere to nowhere suggests that, rather than a dialectical progression of interaction with nature initiated so as to be eventually "transcend[ed]" by an inherently super-natural imagination, the representation of an unidentifiable locus whose only antecedent referent is a "narrow chasm" poses the possibility of "nature" made to "serve" instead, in Kant's words, "as a schema of the supersensible," representing, therein, no visually circumscribed "Gorge" or any other geographical "place," but an "Imagination" as difficult to know as it is to arrive at "knowledge" from "Power." On the dialectical path through and beyond nature, see Hartman's classic "Via Naturaliter Negativa," *Wordsworth's Poetry,* pp. 33–69 (44). On the "empty" symbolism of endtimes required to close a "chasm" whose "represented" contents are as unfathomable as it and the "abyss" of "Imagination" are, citing Wordsworth's theory of poetics, "real," by way of recourse to a gallery of icons that name themselves as such—"Characters of the great Apocalypse,/The Types and symbols of Eternity" (ll. 639–640)—Marchant importantly notes: "Saying that the woods, waterfalls, winds, crags and sky were as characters, types, and

complex, Wordsworth's representation in "real language" of a reality no subject can experience in any purely "empirical" sense, composed of objects at once in constant motion and fixed, is both the culmination of all the experiences of self-alienation whose purposeful enactment within the world his poetry narrates, and the otherworldly representation of the "real" world that brings his theory of poetry, wary of appeals to "imagination," full circle, an unsee-able "scene" which, for that very reason, accurately represents the ever-altering inter-actions enabled by their articulation in acts of language in which all subjects of experience participate. Here Wordsworth offers not even the barest narrativization of that representation: neither a sudden dropping from view of the visible, nor the vanishing between verse stanzas of a "thing" not seen to live in the first place, nor the "fear" or absence of "fears" that correspond to these, powerful though all these are. In the "so-called" "Gondo Gorge" passage that follows it in the purely sequential, or illogical, mode of non sequitur, the "Poet" instead represents the "awful Power" of interaction in and with "real language" properly misnamed "Imagination." For if "Imagination," "so-called by sad incompetence of human speech," is encountered by the common subject of language, of necessity unexpectedly, not "face-to-face" but as an "abyss" within the "mind" itself, what more "fitting" subject, than its negative "Power," of a "scene" in which all knowable boundaries between the perceptible and imaginary are represented as constantly, and so also necessarily imperceptibly, in the course of being transgressed.

Without further comment, or narrative transition back to the travelers, the story line of the poem recommences—"That night our lodging was a House that stood . . ."[22]—as if no "narrow chasm" had been said to have been "entered" (let alone left), and no description of the least delimitable, or "narrow," "scene" imaginable had intervened between "chasm" and "House." Just as the word, "Imagination," resurfaces

---

symbols invests them with a mystique. But possessing a mystique is a lesser thing than being a mystery . . . a new relationship with, or mode of apprehension of, the natural world, a state of being *involving* a mode of understanding. No doubt the fear accompanying the new state prompted a comforting resolution of the superficially incoherent experience, but the one offered *is unworthy of the depth of insight represented by the poetry* of the account of the pass. It is a question of kinds of truth, *the conclusion being not so much unjustifiable as empty*" (*Principles . . .*, p. 30 [emphasis added]).

22. *The Prelude*, V I: 642.

positively conceptualized in specifically *non*-experiential—celestial, spiritualist, divine, harmonic, and other clichéd "poetic"—terms throughout the second half of the poem, after the crossing of the Alps, or, rather, the Peasant's informing the travelers that, contrary to the "hopes" that had guided them, they had indeed already done so without knowing it, the emergence of unanticipated, experiential events recedes from "view" within the "future" narrative "course" of *The Prelude*.[23]

Still, Wordsworth's "so-called" "Gondo Gorge" passage can be understood to produce a certain kind of "knowledge" from a "Power" (necessarily misnamed "Imagination") without saying, and perhaps without knowing it is doing so. For, however incompetent the "speech" in which we do so, any and "every subject" ("jedermann"[24]) of experience whose "mind" encounters and, as only minds unlimited by and to empirical experience can, *reads* Wordsworth's "real" representation of "power" *a posteriori* here, is also capable of "judging" it—in Kant's entirely original, specifically verbal theory of the "power" "to judge"— "sublime," and it is the poetry as much as any "analytic" of the sublime that first permits us to know we can do so. In describing objects severed from our knowledge of them not as they "really are . . . in and for themselves" ("Dinge an sich . . . für sich wirklich"[25]) but as what Kant was also first to call "phenomena," Wordsworth instead "sees," and moreover, gives the reader to "see," these objects, in deed, "as the poets do" ("sehen . . . wie die Dichter es tun"[26]), neither narratively mediating or explaining in advance nor "'recogniz[ing]'" and rewriting them after the fact, but "showing" us, so to speak, "what" it "looks like" when, in Kant's words, "the poet uses the sensible as a schema for the supersensible."[27]

For knowledge of the "power to judge" is also knowledge *of* "Imagination"—not as the artificial "colouring" or cloaking element we

23. *The Prelude*, VI: 850.

24. Kant, *KU* B 20, X: 126.

25. Kant, *KrV*, BXX, III: 27, *et passim*.

26. Kant, *KU* B 119, X: 196. I have analyzed this remarkable observation by Kant, in the "General Remarks" to the "Analytic of the Sublime," that, in order to judge natural phenomena "sublime," we "must see them as the poets do," in *The Imposition of Form* (Princeton: Princeton University Press, 1987), pp. 62–68, and, recently, in *The Linguistic Condition*, Chap. 3, Sec. 3.

27. Kant, KU B 216, X: 265. See *The Linguistic Condition*,, "Preface," and Chap. 3, Sec. 3.

may conceive it to be, but as the ability "to see," in the realest, most material terms, "scenes" in which cognition and perception come into conflict. And, like Wordsworth's "daring" "boy," in the act of reading we not only "see" these "scenes" but actively stage them. For "reading" is *not* an organic requirement of life; it, too, is an addition, an alteration of the natural order of perception that we perform. In the "scene" of "descent," in which down is also up, that the poet-traveler's own heartfelt "hopes" to see a fabled turning point and passage help create through their negation, the "spontaneous overflowing" of power is at the same time "something regular," something "never to be decayed." Without giving any verbal indication that he is "conscious" of doing so, as his travelers continue their journey, Wordsworth, the poet, gets "*there*": to the "real" rather than anticipated turning point in this epic narrative poem of "my life"[28] in which the "true difficulty" of producing "Power" of which "knowledge is the effect" is, in effect, traversed. In representing "Imagination" not by the "poetic" cliché of an angelically detected harmony of the spheres, as he will toward the epic's (and his life's) "Conclusion,"[29] but as "that awful Power" to transgress the perspectival, temporal and spatial rules of scene and image-making—and, specifically, to do so *literally*, i.e., in words without "quotation marks," i.e., without saying so—Wordsworth makes "real language" an integral part of the real compared with which any putatively purely "empirical" record reveals itself a local fiction. The "knowledge" it produces is no passive reflection of either "Matters of Fact" or "of the heart," but the representation of "man and the objects that surround him . . . acting and re-acting upon each other," and the first assumption its use of language disrupts is that which opposes "language" to "what," recalling Kant, "we understand under the word" "real" itself. Similarly, rather than understanding what one "understands under the word" "poetry" as the expression, in purposefully artificial "poetic diction," of *either* "emotion" or "recollection," "experience" *or* "contemplation," "spontaneous power" *or* "mechanical" "habit," and external "sense" *or* "thought," for Wordsworth it is the "real" interaction of all these that every "poet" "worthy of the name" effectively represents.

28. *The Prelude*, I: 69.
29. *The Prelude*, XIV: 98–99.

Part III

Necessary Poetics: Theory of the Real

Chapter 10

"The Real Horizon" (Beyond Emotion): "Living Things" "That Do Not Live Like Living Men," or the "Path" of the Subject Crossed

The following analysis initially came about in response to an invitation to participate in an international conference, entitled "Interiority/ Exteriority," organized by the Yale University German Department. The conference's full title and subtext: "Interiority/Exteriority: Rethinking Emotions," indicate the direct relation between that context and Wordsworth's poetics in their combined conflation of the very spatial and intellectual, and intellectual with affective experiences and activities that Wordsworth's extended definition of poetry instead renders contradictory. Whereas the full colon separating the disproportionate halves of Wordsworth's most complex—and most routinely truncated— definition of how poetry comes about works to demarcate inside from outside, any "spontaneous overflow of feeling" from "act[s]" of internal "contemplation" (thinking or "rethinking") undertaken "at length," as well as, and, above all, "feeling" itself from the "modify[ing]" "representati[on]" of "past feeling" by "thoughts"—"For all good poetry is the spontaneous overflow of powerful feelings: *and though* this be true, Poems to which any value can be attached were never produced on any variety of subjects but by a man who, being possessed of more than usual organic sensibility, had also thought long and deeply[1]"— the colon that, in the conference's title, instead equates an experiential

---

1. See Owen and Smyser, I: 127, for the full extension of Wordsworth's complex definition, and I: 149, for its later recapitulation within the "Preface." See Part I, Chap. 4 of this study for a detailed analysis of Wordsworth's openly self-contradictory definition, including its direct representation of the division between "feeling" and "thought" constitutive not only of poetry but of any "understanding" of thought and feeling themselves, as, the poet-theorist observes, of anything "really important to men."

spatial division ("Interiority/Exteriority") with an elision of all such differentiation, as between progressive and reflective acts of contemplation and the spontaneous "emotions" they take as their object, was summarily encapsulated by the personifying metaphor, lacking any possible object, of a "language of emotions," reflexively employed by conference organizers and participants throughout the discussions that ensued. While consistent with recent academic interest in the multipurpose, amorphous quality-*cum*-object, "affect," itself precipitated by the evacuation of both thinking and representation by flattening appeals to an equally undefined quality-*cum*-subject, "power," cribbed by poor, anthropomorphizing metaphor, from the physical forces constitutive of empirical nature, the notion of a "language" whose subject *or* object would be "emotions" articulates its own unwitting contradiction as such. Having taken some pains in recent work to describe the material, historical *and* arbitrary, which is to say, conventionally enabled means of demarcating interiority from exteriority in actual space, and to distinguish spatially constructed notions of inside and outside from emotion especially, as well as from their converse, fictions of so-called "inner" "sensation" invented to circumvent the difficulty of theorizing the often conflicting internal acts and processes that, alternately enabling and disabling, formative and deforming, work to compose, compare and mediate events of sensory "perception" in the first place, I wondered, in a sense, "where" any discussion of emotions conceived instead in terms equating space with language and representational abstraction with fleeting affect should or could begin.

As if to demonstrate the unpredictability of the innumerable ways perception and intellection *interact*, what came to my mind uninvited at that time was a strange and enduringly inexplicable phrase of Proust, whom I was then teaching: a simple but unfathomable noun phrase that seemed to provide an indication of what considerations of either interiority or exteriority—of either a pure, supposedly noncognitive emotionality or pure, supposedly noncognitive spatiality, no less than their identification or conflation—disfigure and miss. That phrase, "the real horizon," is, to begin with, a contradiction in terms—all horizons being situational illusions, there is no such thing. Yet since there is no one, one could say, who knows this better than Proust—no one keener on the distinction, and devoted to telling the story of distinguishing, between mere appearances and the real—it seemed to me that it was neither a putative "inner" nor actual "outer" "space," no "here" nor "there," just as it was no emotive affect or physical phenomenon Proust had "in mind." Whatever he had "in" mind, when writing of a "horizon" to which our perceptual spatialization of space, as of experience, did not pertain, seemed instead, very much in the manner of Lukács' rendering of the proleptic progress of literary history, the answer to a question I did not know yet how to ask.[2]

The program of the Yale conference bore as proviso or motto a single, memorable quote from Paul de Man which, standing in direct critical relation to its title while never discussed during the conference proceedings, hovered above it like an allegorical superscript: "[Literary] criticism stands under the aegis of an inside/outside metaphor that is never being seriously questioned." Just as such plainly self-contradictory metaphors as "rethinking emotions" and a "language of emotions" continue to orient current discourses on literature, culture, and history, without serious question, whatever de Man had in mind, in suggesting a different, distinctly non-metaphorical direction for literary criticism, remained, like the nonfigurative experiences of interiority and exteriority that literature might instead, on his view, be precisely purposed to express, remained sealed off from analysis, at that meeting of investigative minds, like a mystical allegory from the worldly methods of *hermeneusis*. Before exploring some of the descriptions of emotions, interiority and exteriority that indeed made some sense to him, I took that banner citation from de Man neither as an article of belief nor self-evident truism but literal indication that it was with him which any consideration of a non-"metaphorical" or "real horizon" might best begin.

Simply if paradoxically put: Paul de Man abhorred talk of "feelings," but he abhorred the use and promotion of bad metaphors, freshly minted or clichéd, even more. The reasons for this are no secret, and hardly mysterious. Simply, declaratively and nonparadoxically put: talking *about* feelings debased both language *and* feeling, in his view, by missing the compelling reason and real consequences of each, while the *bavardage* of bad metaphors helped spread the mystifications engendered by the former around, ultimately promoting one, thoroughly mystified and mystifying feeling in particular, that of personal ambition, described in Rüdiger Campe's contribution to the conference[3] as an all-encompassing desire for personal superiority, a narcissism whose own

---

2. See Georg Lukács, *Die Theorie des Romans*, Berlin: Cassirer, 1920.

3. Cf. Rüdiger Campe, "Presenting the Affect: The Scene of Pathos in Aristotle's Rhetoric and its Revision in Descartes' *Passions of the Soul*," in R. Campe and Julia Weber, eds., *Rethinking Emotion* (Berlin: de Gruyter, 2015), pp. 37–56.

gratification and self-perpetuation depends upon, fabricates, and enforces hierarchy. Writing about the fatal interdependence of personal self-preservation and aggrandizement promoted by opportunistic alliances within the *huis clos* of hierarchical court society, Mme de Lafayette memorably designated this all-encompassing desire for personal superiority "l'esprit glorieux." The nearly inevitable phenomenological extension of such a *personally* glorifying "esprit" into *inter*personal ambition is one manifestation of what de Man called ideology. Any notion of an objectified language of emotions would be an expression only of ideology and a prime candidate for de Man's critique for two important reasons. First, such a "language" would purport to report and so justify the research of something that does not in fact exist, and, thus, secondly, it must obscure our understanding of the two terms it metaphorically relates: language, on the one hand, and emotions, on the other. In the partly deictic, partly abstract terms whose metaphoric use de Man questioned, the self-contradictory notion of a "language of emotions" employs a similarly figurative, prepositional shorthand to conflate "exteriority"—language as perceptible sign or symbol; as sensorially rendered code of some kind—with "interiority," or whatever we do that is *not* immediately, phenomenally manifested in and by the act involved (thinking, imagining, remembering, supposing, understanding, deceiving and discovering, to name a few such actions, as well as the full range of feelings and desires accompanying these).

Now the body presents some involuntary manifestations of feelings, such as blushing, shaking, or trembling, but even these typical give-aways, perceptible betrayals of corporeal quickening, can, like any other, be brought under control, mastered in time. Perhaps we didn't need Mme de Lafayette, Racine, Rousseau, Diderot, Laclos, Kleist, Keats, Balzac, Baudelaire, Stendhal, or Proust to tell us this, but the French literary tradition in particular would hardly exist, let alone instruct and reflect every moment of our social lives, without its acknowledgement of that fact. The occurrence of the same "tell-tale" signs, or unwilled indications of feeling, can, however, also be feigned—as all good *and* bad writing, good *and* bad acting, and good *and* bad social interactions remind us—making it hard if not impossible to tell "real" feeling from simulated, the presence from the absence of what Richardson and Wordsworth called "involuntary motions," those movements of mind and body we do not control and so rightly, metaphorically call movings outward, "e-motions."

This is not to say that there are no external indications of emotion that *remain* involuntary, including, not least of all, indications of one's own anxiety as to whether one's studied concealment of emotion will succeed. Professional gamblers call these "tells"—the physical "tics" that, upon repetition, are the recognizable signs of a player bluffing, i.e., lying about the real state and quality of the hand he is playing, "betting the house," as they say, on a house of cards—a paper valuation, as they say on the market. Professional gamblers or not, we all know "tells" eventually— or should know them—when we see them; without them the so-called game of life would hardly be a game or be life, let alone of any vital, rather than merely acquisitive interest to the players. Since without them, all social or interpersonal life would be replaced by the ideological pursuit of emotion always practically inseparable from the desire for absolute power, as well as its real-world corollary, the so-called natural law of appropriation and annihilation of the other otherwise known as war, luckily for us some tells just keep on telling—if we bother to look for them, to *see instead of feeling.* Even Paul de Man was subject to such a purely physical, in his case optical tell of involuntary motion, although, since this tell, or, in Diderot's terms, this "external symptom" of feeling, *was* truly involuntary, one could never identify or objectify with certainty the emotion it signaled; and de Man, conscious of it, was even more conscious of the fact there was nothing he could do about it, and so instead took as much pleasure in calling attention to it—its implacable naturalism—as in citing its non-natural, or literary precedent. (The tell was an abrupt and total change in eye color; the literary prototype, a particularly appearance-conscious character, plagued by such an unmasterable physical tell, in Proust—M. Legrandin.)

As subject to them as anyone—that is, as any of us not entirely hollowed out by the sole controlling motive of self-aggrandizement, the flattening process necessitated for the projection of the self on to the big screen of one's own imagining—de Man recognized, and, in rare instances, went so far as to thematize the fact, that this particular variable in his particular corporeal composition would, upon a sudden, give him away, commenting on it with apparent happiness, which is to say, in full ironic mode and non-ironic relief that such involuntary signals, shorn of code and convention—i.e., of language—happen at all.

Yet, while constating as much—that our bodies can tell others that we feel something, something that affects our, properly amorphously termed, "state of mind"; and stating even, as de Man's rare self-commentary suggested, thank goodness or givenness for that—we should also confirm that neither such involuntary, physiological tells nor studied and fungible signs of emotion could ever constitute a language, or languages, not even for a single subject, let alone the infinite number of individual subjects to whom infinitely specific and fleeting experiences of feelings are given. It is not that feelings and language are not *both* terribly effective: they are, one can accurately say, inestimably effective. It is their metaphorical yoking together that papers over that effectivity, postponing the understanding of the effects of language *and* of feeling upon us until a scientistically reified language of language, or complacently reified feeling of feeling, is proposed to take its place, pushing the proverbial ball down the road to nowhere but the prolonged evasion of understanding again.

The metaphoric combination of language and feeling into a language of feeling will indeed always subdivide into the language of language, posited as a scientifically confirmable object, and the feeling of feeling, posited as a prelinguistic and postcritical object, happily available, however, to endless pronouncements on its behalf. These pure positings of objective positivity where there is no positive object to begin with, belong, of course, to a recognizable species of metaphor—catachresis—but with an added twist. They objectify, through either hyper-logical over-methodologicization, or the belle-lettristic non-method of free association, an object that isn't one by naming it for *another* object that isn't one. Just to indicate how universally and pragmatically useful such double catachreses can be, how equally welcomed, indeed vaunted, even by openly divergent political programs, it is worth noting that this procedure for compounding fiction with fiction, for making tautology seem not tautological, but defiant, indeed singularly courageous, has been used by successive, supposedly opposed American presidents, who, with the same visible flash of self-satisfaction, have described their successively opposing courses of action as acts of "doubling down." Lifted from the parlance of professional gamblers, "to double down" does not mean to build upon strength, insight, or understanding, or even to hedge one's bets or "cover" one's—uncertain—"position," but, rather, just the opposite, to compound one's bluff by adding wager to wager, wedding fabrication with evasion by a single, indissoluble bond.

Just as purely metaphoric ascriptions of language to emotions and emotions to language combine the two into one doubly non-existent, and so limitlessly exploitable, object of discourse, a verbal association, which, referable back only to the *verba* of which it is composed, is thus doubly shielded both from internal scrutiny and external comparison with anything else, so the familiar opposition of internal to external is one whose conception de Man questioned—not because the difference between them has no bearing on the life of the body and, part of and different from all other parts of the body, the mind, but, on the contrary, because the facile exclusion or usurpation of one by the other facilitates the mischaracterization and misunderstanding of both and their relation. Spatializing metaphors commemorating the "depths of interiority" do little if anything to describe or follow out what happens when we think, and/or feel, and/or know. Instead they further conceal these, and will continue to, even as we develop their converse, the image-technology made to make externally visible, in attractive color-coded pictures, the working of every neural synapse and chemical reaction "in" the brain. Spatial images suggesting we have an "inside" that we can locate, track, and turn "outside," and whose activity we may thus observe as we might observe the translucent bodies of single-cell organisms subdivide, delude us not only in excluding from consideration our mind's relentless invention of and reliance upon semiotic and graphic media—external forms that we, our minds and bodies, make—but in occluding, moreover, the way in which our "interiority" is intensely subject to all forms of exteriority, especially those we do not and could not make.

There is an outside—Wordsworth made this clearest—and when we discover and recognize this, often at the very instigation of our internal selves, it does not stay "outside," as an object of perception and spur to classifiable emotion, but gets mixed up with, changes, disrupts, displaces, and so makes questionable whatever that mental "inside" keeps stored within it, including our conception that what "is" inside is our very own storage facility, or facilitator: an archive. Just as Wordsworth, conventionally considered a nature poet, makes nature stop appearing as the nature we know—the external world through which we, as feeling, cognizing, and desiring subjects, move—and compels it instead to seem to move *through* a subject formerly neatly divided between internal desire and external goal, so a "real" rather than imagined "inside" and "outside" would be as different as "here" and "there," when "there" is where all life as we perceive and know it ends, and the "horizon" we can see before us is interrupted by another, unforeseeable exteriority.

When, as discussed in Part I, Chapter 6, the boy agent and first-person subject of Book I of Wordsworth's autobiographical *Prelude* is narrated to steal a rowboat, so as to traverse a delimited expanse of water, keeping his "view" "fixed" upon "the horizon" visible before him, while rowing, phenomenologically speaking, backwards, toward a "point" lying behind him, in the direction opposite to that he faces, the poet represents him(self) confronted by a reality at which he could never aim his action, as he sees that widening horizon vanish and something unknown come into view, something, furthermore, unknowable because inextricable from its own "motion":

> . . . like one who rows,
> Proud of his skill, to reach a chosen point
> With an unswerving line, I fixed my view
> Upon the summit of a craggy ridge,
> The horizon's utmost boundary . . .
> When, from the craggy steep till then
> The horizon's bound, a huge peak, black and huge,
> As if with voluntary power instinct
> Upreared its head. I struck and struck again,
> And growing still in stature the grim shape
> Towered up between me and the stars, and still,
> For so it seemed, with purpose of its own
> And measured motion like a living thing
> Strode after me . . .[4]

As if Wordsworth's most famous and least examined definition of poetry had itself been *mise en scène*, his poetic subject crosses a phenomenal horizon between subjective emotion and the "measured motion" of something "like a living thing" proceeding "with purpose of its own." Like the full colon dividing the immediacy of "feeling" of the first part of Wordsworth's extended narrative definition of poetry in the "Preface" ("Poetry is . . .:) from its contradiction ("and though this be true, . . ."[5]) and replacement by "thoughts" whose "continuation" proceeds "mechanically," by force of "repetition,"[6] the "line" crossed by the boy's "fix[ing]" of a "point" on a then apparent "horizon" to serve as counterpoint to his own purposeful motion, suddenly becomes as "real" a barrier to conception as any "living thing" in "seem[ing]" pursuit of him, precisely in its being irreversibly destroyed. After seeing "that spectacle," a scene definitively outside him, the boy experiences the negation of all the "familiar" images and attributes of nature he had maintained inside him: "for many days, my brain/Worked with a dim and undetermined sense . . . No familiar shapes/Remained, no pleasant images of trees,/Of sea or sky, no colours of green fields."[7] These "images"

---

4. *The Prelude* [1850], I: 377–85.

5. For the full citation of that definition, see Part I, Chap. 4, n. 5, n. 7.

6. Ibid.

7. *The Prelude* [1850], I: 391–97.

of things and perceptions of and names for "colours" are not replaced by other, newly minted words and images but cancelled through and through, by "unknown modes of being"[8] that, instead of serving to refurbish his mental archive, "move slowly through the mind," and do so *unlike* him, with neither horizon in sight nor the eyes to see one.

A terrifying, because truly foreign externality, perceptible as "growing still" even as one moves *away* from it in space, destroys the fundamentally spatial model of perception on which notions of a conscious, volitional or psychological "inside" and an unconscious, involuntary or empirical "outside" rest. In direct opposition to the perceptual "horizon" on which he "fixed [his] view," the "measured motion" of the "thing" the boy perceives does *not* move in function of the boy's own ("stroke after stroke"), and the non-perceptual or real horizon it crosses is instead that of the perceiving subject itself. For, a "living thing" perceived to "grow" and move toward its viewer cannot be perceived and cognized with the aid of consciousness as a finite object in space. No longer a demonstrable external object nor subject of internal apperception, the "thing" whose motion is as visibly as it is internally disorienting acts upon the boy to supplant the initial act of its external perception or render perception somehow external to itself, replacing both "familiar shapes" and the brief "spectacle" of their usurpation with something that succeeds them once that perception is out of "sight." Unlike a stolen boat that can be returned to its proper place— "left" "[t]here in her mooring-place" after, "with trembling oars," the boy has "stole[n] [his] way" back to shore— that something is no longer a "living" "strid[ing]" "thing," terrifying because at once both disorienting *and* perceptible, but something or things still ongoing that the boy does not see, "forms" of "unknown modes of being" that he instead retains a mental "sense of," and whose own landscape, scene or stage the boy's "mind" now unwillingly provides: "but after I had seen /That spectacle, for many days, my brain/Worked with a dim and undetermined sense of unknown modes of being ... huge and mighty forms, that do not live/Like living men moved slowly through the mind/By day, and were a trouble to my dreams."[9]

The "horizon" the boy kept before his eyes while rowing, back first, into the opposite direction— the coordination, in the visible shape of a line, of his motion through and position in space at any moment— epitomizes the view of exteriority by which we orient ourselves at all

8. *The Prelude* [1850], I: 393.
9. *The Prelude* [1850], I: 390–400.

times. It is the line that delimits what is outside us, as far as the eye can see, until, using something not ours to begin with—a stolen or borrowed rowboat, in this, at first glance, conventionally pastoral context, or some other external medium, tool or implement for altering or "rewriting," either in reality or in effect, the visible relation between our bodily position in space and that of the bodies around us—we move closer to a "chosen point" or goal, and our "horizon" of vision is suddenly effaced by something before or behind it, something that had always been "there," i.e., outside us, but that we did not, indeed, could not see before our combination of linear motion with a fixed "point" of vision began. What Wordsworth makes plain is that the "natural" ability to see an external "horizon" in front of and outside us is vulnerable not to its own ultimate exhaustion—there will always be another temporary field of vision, another delimitation of the external by an horizon whenever we look out and move at the same time—but, rather, to the passions that get us moving, or rowing, in the first place: the "troubled pleasure," as Wordsworth calls it, with which, unknowingly, and by supplemental means of our own making or appropriation, we see not a new horizon but something whose own motion brings with it the horizon's demise, not only in the sense of what we can see before us, but in the sense of the inherently permeable (i.e., nongeometrical) line demarcating "inside" from "outside" the mind. Poetic agency, the ability to *act* that each of Wordsworth's definitions of poetry describes, is no Promethean capacity to create life from inanimate matter but the capacity to interact with the material world in such a way that, as we "do" so, the "scenes" composed and horizons created by our perceptions of it are crossed.

Chapter 11

"The Real Horizon" (Before Emotion): What Proust (Rousseau, Diderot, and Hegel) Had "in" Mind

In direct contrast to the graphic clarity, and abrupt conclusion, of Wordsworth's vivid narrative description of a visible "horizon" effaced, Proust's enigmatic phrase, "the real horizon," appears barely connected to the tightly interwoven threads of depiction and speculation that precede it, the well-known section of *Du côté de chez Swann* containing the narrator's observations on the Vices and Virtues of Giotto. One of the richest compositional sequences in the entire novel, proceeding, as if seamlessly, from diachronic narration to mimetic description, to non-mimetic symbolic theory, hermeneutics and poetics, to theory of the novel and autobiographical reflection, this justly celebrated section begins, concretely enough, with the narrator's recollection of the resemblance, first "pointed out to him" by Swann, between one in the "succession" of family kitchenmaids in Combray and one of the subjects of Giotto's allegorical series in Padua.[1] It referentially describes the subject matter specifically depicted in the paintings themselves before proceeding to consider the appearance and effectiveness of all painted *or* natural symbols; the materiality and "thought" content of symbols in general; the "impenetrable" "pieces of opacity" that are part of any "real being"; the "discovery" by novelists of a way to "replace" these; and finally, his own discovery that he himself has always been himself, at every "moment" of his life, all of a piece, united immaterially "in a same, unbending outpouring of all the forces of my life" ("un même et infléchissable jaillissement de toutes les forces de ma vie").[2]

---

1. Marcel Proust, *A la recherche du temps perdu*, 3 vols. Paris: Bibliothèque de la Pléiade, I: 80. All translations from the French are my own.

2. Ibid. I: 80–87.

Little could serve as a less fitting prelude to "the real horizon" the narrator then names, and perhaps it was exactly its own discrete divergence from the perfectly integrated "outpouring" of fiction and reflection succeeding which it is casually named, that made the notion of a "real," as opposed to imputed, "horizon" cross my mind as I tried to imagine what—other than a compounded catachresis—an horizonless yet deictically indicated spatialization of emotion, let alone spatialized *language* of emotions, might be. Before turning to the question of what, for Proust, a "real," or nonperspectival "horizon" could possibly be or mean—a limit as independent of human narrative and reflection, as language is of space, and both language and space are of emotion—it is worth considering another putative, signally instructive horizon described in explicit relation to language: the specular boundary in face of which Rousseau places the origin of language "within" a perceiving subject.

In the posthumously published *Essay on the Origin of Languages* (*Essai sur l'origine des langues* [written 1740s? 1750s?]), Rousseau asserts the two following propositions: first, that language could only have arisen due to "moral" rather than "physical" "needs," which, by contrast, can instead be expressed adequately by physical gestures and expressions alone; and, second, that the "first language," in being motivated by "moral needs" or "passions," had to have been "figural," while the "true name" and "proper meaning" of "objects" were "invented" *after* them.[3] One assumes, Rousseau notes, that such a sequence of events is impossible, "since a figure consists only in the translation of the sense" or "idea" signified by a word; "otherwise," he states correctly, "figural language would mean nothing" ("autrement le langage figuré ne signifierait rien"[4]). In order to explain this unconventional sequencing of intellectual events, Rousseau offers, in the mode of demonstration necessitated by his and any critically logical, or anti-positivist, theoretical writing, a hypothetical narrative "example."[5] Rather than attempt to demonstrate his assertion of the priority and figural expression of the passions on the basis of a known given (whose own cognitive content, as example, would thus *per force* be available to doubt), Rousseau begins from an experience of a given unknown. Likewise, rather than confuse the construction and workings of language with the inherently

3. Jean-Jacques Rousseau, *Essai sur l'origine des langues, où il est parlé de la mélodie et de l'imitation musicale,* ed. Charles Porset (Paris: Nizet, 1969), Chap. II and III, pp. 41–47.

4. Rousseau, *Essai,* p. 68.

5. Ibid.

nonreferential laws of logic, the logical sequence he narrates refers to subjects and objects encountering each other, in a scene delimited by their encounter, for the "first" (i.e., "pre"-linguistic) time. The succinct story he tells links language to ignorance and a motivating error of perception originating not in empirical reality but the blinding effect of passion upon perception. Acknowledging the reasonable question of his "reader" as to how "an expression can be figural before having a proper sense," Rousseau "respond[s] with an example" of how the internal rather than external determination of a word, the "idea" rather than reality behind it, causes it to be articulated first:

> The savage (or natural) man, in encountering others will at first be frightened. His fear will have made him see these men larger and stronger than himself; he will have given them the name *Giants*. After many experiences, he will have recognized that these supposed Giants, being neither bigger nor stronger than he, did not agree in their stature with the idea he had first attached to the word Giant. Thus he will invent another name common to them and to himself, such as, for example, the name *man*, and he will leave that of *Giant* to the false object that struck him during his illusion. That is how the figural word is born before the proper word, when passion fascinates the eyes and the first idea that it offers to us is not that of the truth.

> [Un homme sauvage en rencontrant d'autres se sera d'abord effrayé. Sa frayeur lui aura fait voir ces hommes plus grands et plus forts que lui-même; il leur aura donné le nom de *Géans*. Après beaucoup d'expériences il aura reconnu que ces prétendus Géans n'étant ni plus grands ni plus forts que lui, leur stature ne convenoit point à l'idée qu'il avoit d'abord attaché au mot de Géant. Il inventera donc un autre nom commun à eux et à lui, tel, par exemple, que le nom d'*homme*, et laissera celui de Géant à l'objet faux qui l'avoit frappé durant son illusion. Voilà comment le mot figuré naît avant le mot propre, lorsque la passion nous fascine les yeux et que la première idée qu'elle nous offre n'est pas celle de la vérité.[6]

6. Rousseau, *Essai*, p. 47. This particular passage from Rousseau rebuts *both* common literalist and logical positivist views of the basis and purpose of language *and* the description of a nonlinguistic "fascination" exercised by images upon perceiving subjects that is put forth by Blanchot (See Maurice Blanchot, *The Space of Literature*, trans. Ann Smock [Lincoln: University of Nebraska Press, 1982], p. 32 [Paris, 1955, p. 28]; see also Brigitte Weingart's essay,

Rousseau's story of one man first seeing others may appear to offer strong, if strictly narrative support for the notion that the identification of a "language of emotions" is not only not a necessary misidentification but the real and proper identity of language itself, as long as we consent to the notion that language is figural first, denotative second. Yet the problem with even that enlightened view of what Rousseau is describing has to do with his own version, in this "example," of Wordsworth's fictive but no less visible "horizon." Rousseau does not explicitly spatialize his example, plotting it geometrically, as Wordsworth does, onto the rectilinear axis of vision approaching its delimitation in the perceived perpendicular axis of an horizon. Neither are an "act of stealth" and desired progression toward "a chosen point" at the origin of Rousseau's scene. This is because the fictive "subject" of Rousseau's "example" is not yet a subject in deed; unlike Wordsworth's past "I," this purely nominal subject does not "fix" his "vision" upon any "chosen point" nor see objects and their spatial interrelations in figurative, geometrical terms. One thing is instead as insignificant as another, equivalent and indifferent except insofar as it can be immediately consumed or used, and space as such immaterial to this dormant "subject," theoretical twin of the

---

"Contact at a Distance," entitled for Blanchot's description of "fascination," in *Rethinking Emotion*, pp. 73–100 [esp. 95–97]). While Blanchot's definition of fascination, as a "passion for the image," endows the image with the capacity to fix our "vision" in a "dead gaze" that "never comes to an end" (*Space. . .*, p. 32), Rousseau's remarkable reference to distinct moments "quand la passion fascine les yeux" ("when passion fascinates our eyes") locates the source of fascination not in the image but in the "passion" that, originating in the subject, colors our vision. Similarly, the direct object of our "fascinat[ing]" passion is the "eye" that sees images, not images as such. This reversal of conventional cause and effect, typical, perhaps, for Rousseau, contradicts nearly all contemporary thinking about, indeed fascination with "the image." To use Rousseau's own term, such misidentifications of the source of our fascination "transfers" a power from its origin in the passions to inanimate pictures of dispassionate objects, imagining images and objects themselves to be the magical source of our fascination with them. In this Rousseau's analysis of the "origin of language" most closely resembles Kant's ("Copernican") reversal of our understanding of the "beautiful" and "sublime" as originating not in objects as such but in the noncognitive "feeling of pleasure" and "pain" issuing in verbal acts of judgment realized by subjects. See this study, Chap. 2, n. 6; *The Linguistic Condition*, Chap. 2, Sec. 4, and Chap. 3, Sec. 3 esp.

"natural" or "savage man" of Rousseau's Second Discourse. Thus, its external "horizon" is not the visible line that actively cognizing subjects carry, so to speak, "within" them—a projected spatial demarcation erased only by "unknown and mighty forms" that cross it as the line of our corresponding axis of vision lengthens—but rather an intellectual limit first made visible within immediately familiar surroundings by an especially disturbing appearance of the unknown. Distinctive in the uncanny sense that it appears both foreign *and* familiar, similar to a subject *before* that subject has any conception of itself, the occurrence of such an uncustomary appearance would give rise not only to the not quite specular notion of an unknown other, "Giant," but to that of a continuously subjectively delimited "horizon," too, as the absence of any distinction between inside and outside, "here" and "there," is overwritten and overridden by the inaugural perception of another subject, the one now over there, visible to and opposite me, who must come from a newly discovered "outside," the land of what I do not "know," nor, till this, its appearance in questionable relation to me, ever thought about before. On this view, the subject of a so-called "language of emotion" that first utters the objective fiction or "trope," "Giant," would also cognize and define the new-found concept of an horizon as the line apparently dividing consciousness from all (it now knows) it doesn't know.

Rousseau's narrative, however, includes the passage of time that proves this language to be in error. "After many experiences" ("après beaucoup d'expériences"), the natural man who "invents the first language" as originary projection or trope recognizes and amends this error, Rousseau states. Alluding, by one of the most effective litotes in the history of modern philosophy, to what may as well be considered all of human history, Rousseau leaves the content of these "many" ensuing "experiences" undefined. Yet, given the absence of any common language between them, the mutual "experiences" of Rousseau's exemplary "man" and his other are more likely to have been violently conflictual than coolly comparative: to have been so impassioned, in other words, as to have culminated in the single *purely* material grounds for comparison, that of measuring one's own stature, after the fact, against that of an immobile corpse. Whatever the content of those "many experiences," the empirical error in perception they succeed results in the creation not of one but two literal terms: the trope "Giant" subdivides into "giant," meaning a remarkably or unnaturally big man, and "man," meaning someone—some other one—who is just like me after all. In other words, "the first language" would not be a language without, at least, two to speak it, i.e., until its simultaneous doubling within and by another subject—the same irresolubly circular problem, of language requiring language to become language, and subjects requiring relations to other subjects to become subjects, that Rousseau lays out in three clearly stated paradoxes in the Second Discourse (*Discourse on the Foundations of Inequality*[7])—and that same doubleness of production must extend to its semantic dimension, too.

Were it instead to remain a singular, nontemporal, and undivided event, unrelated to referential "experiences," the hypothetical "figural" "origin" of language represented here by Rousseau—the first-encounter formation of an impassioned "trope" for an object somehow known while unknown—would, ironically enough, be roughly equivalent to the classically "natural" account of the origin of language in song (and identification of song with feeling) reiterated by Herder in his later *Essay on the Origin of Language* (*Abhandlung über den Ursprung der Sprache* [1772]). On this prototypical account of language as sensuous extension—one whose severing and negation by the referential experience of time is the consuming subject of, among others', all Keats' poetry and poetic reflection—the only "authentic" language would indeed be a "language of emotion" indistinguishable from poetry during a "golden age" in which all human utterances constituted spontaneous "musical" outpourings subsequently "lost" to a literal language of rationally purposed conceptual designations. Extending to the gay animism of Nietzsche and, in part, the eruptive ontology of Heidegger on the one hand, and the happy Hobbesianism of Hume, and super-Hume-ian, totalizing historicism of Foucault on the other, the reception of the resulting story line would bifurcate between a decrying of "authentic" truth concealed or a commendation of false beliefs dispelled by scientific method and nomenclature, in short, by negative or positive representations of the conventional, superficial tale of "enlightenment" we all "know"—and Rousseau would have had no "reason" to be the paranoid he was.

Yet, while externally reflective of the story of the birth and development of language Rousseau tells, no account could be further than these fundamentally naturalist descriptions, of an "authentic" "language of emotion," from the relation of language to emotion that Rousseau's story represents. For what neither the figural term, "Giant," nor either of the comparatively defined literal terms, "man" and "giant,"

---

7. See Rousseau, *Discours sur l'origine et les fondements de l'inégalité, op. cit.*, pp. 203–204 esp.

articulates, is the passion engendered by the singular first encounter that produces them in temporally staggered fashion. "Fear"—the motive emotion to which the false object-designation, "Giant," originally responded—remains, before and "after much experience," or at every stage of Rousseau's parallel accounts of the figural to literal formation of language and "illus[ory]" to "true" formation of knowledge, entirely unperceived by its subject, and thus unnamed. Rousseau, unsurpassed theorist of the passions, situates passions at the origin of language, the origin of the unknown, in which both the possibility *and* the limit and horizon of knowledge also first come into view. Like Kant's subject of judgment, Rousseau's "natural man" first *becomes* "man" in speech originating in a positive or negative feeling *it does not name*, occasioned by an encounter with something that it "knows" *it does not know.*[8] Instead of "I"—the similarly unstated subject of the action that Kant calls aesthetic *"judgment"*—and rather than emitting either "natural" shrieks of fear or movements of flight, Rousseau's not-yet "I"—"savage" or "natural man"—enacts what Rousseau calls *"language,"* "name[s]" referring to someone or something outside its ken. Furthermore, in relating the formation and "communicability" of language to the historical formation of not only all arts and sciences but all political and social relations, rather than depicting it to mirror the internally calculable and thus predictable realm of physically generated ratios of force, Rousseau, like Kant, knows that any language, figural or literal, can only be a language, a means of conveying "ideas," if it names things and attributes of things, objects and qualities, *outside* the form of language itself. The progress from trope to proper designation keeps language and the new-found division between inside and outside intact. It is "moral needs," "passions," or "feelings," themselves triggered by an objective encounter with one's own ignorance, that result, first, in impersonal tropes ("Giant," "beautiful," "sublime") substituting for their personal experience, and, only later, in the empirical revision of those tropes and invention of proper or literal terms, abstract concepts, comparative modifiers, and identifying nomenclature—in short, in the development of language as language, the articulate vehicle for the combination and comparison of "ideas" themselves necessarily without distinct, material identity because independent of and thus attachable to any "subject" or "object." To name the internal experience that necessitates this development would instead redefine *all* designations as neither conventionally literal nor arbitrarily "proper" names but errors,

8. See *The Linguistic Condition,* Chap. 2, Secs 3 and 4 esp.

all visibility, *in so far as it appears meaningful,* to be a falsifying projection of what one feels.

Instead of leading us to name what we see either when "passion fascinates our eyes," *or* "after many experiences," when plural bases of comparison have clarified our "view" of things, feelings, if externalized as both origin and object of language, would, on Rousseau's account, end language before it began. To talk about the internal experiences from which words necessarily unnaturally or "improperly" arise, would be to do away with the actual "objectivity" or communicability of any words or signs, and thus the very possibility of all representation, let alone talk. In addition, in short-circuiting the attribution of sense to the objects that occasion it, the naming of the feeling, "fear," as if it were itself an identifiable object, would only name one's own experience of it and not another's, at only one particular moment, and so not even name "fear" in general but what it is "I" feel right now. The language that begins with ignorance, impassioned perceptual error, and trope must bury rather than name the passion with which it identifies an object *as* an object and the outside as delimited by an horizon for the first time, if it is ever to take, however aberrantly, objectified, perceptible, comparable and thus historical, sense-bearing form.

If, following the analysis of the most "truth[ful]," because openly concealing, epistemologist of the passions, Rousseau, any "language of emotion" is in fact *not* a language *of emotion* but of *objects* already misperceived, by a subject who can only perceive and name objects accurately when, those objects now well within his or her horizon, the emotion aroused by the encounter with them has died, and knowledge, including theoretical knowledge, has replaced it, then the impossibility of a language of emotion *a priori*—that is, even as displaced and concealed in object-related tropes—is stated most unequivocally and literally by Rousseau's own "other" and *semblable,* Diderot. The first modern art critic, whose contemporary criticism provided the model for Baudelaire's *Salons,* Diderot is a natural favorite among art historians who value his emphasis upon expressive physiognomy and gesture. His language theory, however, while requiring external manifestations, reveals precisely what expressive physiognomy and even the very notion of self-evident, synchronic painting conceal: the nonphenomenal, "metaphoric" transfers of meaning, caused by the "decomposition" of the senses, that are described to constitute language in its origin in Diderot's *Letter on the Blind, As Used by Those Who See* (*Lettre sur les aveugles à l'usage de ceux qui voient* [1749]), and the "pile of hieroglyphs" left behind by poets attempting to "paint after the moving tableau of the soul" with which they, like Baudelaire's modern painter, cannot keep pace, that is described in the first Letter's decomposed counterpart, the *Letter on the Deaf and Mute, As Used by Those Who Speak and Hear* (*Lettre sur les sourds et muets à l'usage de ceux qui entendent et qui parlent* [1751]).[9]

Nothing could be less transparent and less synchronic than the working relationship between interiority and expressive language defined by Diderot throughout all his writings, from the overtly and covertly theoretical, to the overtly and covertly fictional (theory and fiction being modes of discourse which, in Diderot as in Rousseau, must intersect in coming into existence in the first place).[10] There is language and there are noncognitive emotions in Diderot, but for emotions to be conveyed by a language, for a language of emotions to be perceived to exist, that language and those emotions must be, he asserts, divorced completely. This division is effected not to keep one's interiority—one's feelings—intact, but, rather, because no language could ever be formed and performed by someone who "has" feelings at all. The language of emotion must originate in an ability to look outside, and this ability, Diderot sensibly argues, is strongest in someone with no inside. That apparent paradox, of full expressivity attained and exercised when there is nothing imperceptible, nothing "inside" to express, renders the notion of the language of emotions an oxymoron—that is, so long as one conceives of emotions as actually occurring, as motions within the self that move outward from the self, rather than as objectified externally, in observations, representations, books.

The oxymoron of the language of emotion is what Diderot calls the "paradox of the actor." As described in his great theoretical dialogue

9. Denis Diderot, *Ouevres complètes,* 25 vols, ed. Herbert Dieckmann, Jean Fabre, Jacques Proust, with Jean Varloot (Paris: Hermann, 1975–), IV: 41, 140, 161, 169. (Cf. "Diderot's Adjectives," Chap. 2, Sec. 7, *The Linguistic Condition.*)

10. For a more extensive discussion of the view, articulated throughout Diderot's theoretical as well as fictional works, that it is precisely the *non*-coincidence, not to say mutual exclusion, of interiority and exteriority, or internal experience (whether of cognition, imagination, emotion, or the "soul") and external experience (whether of the "body," the "senses," or the "sign"), that first makes any effective "expression," "language" or "sign," let alone the evocation *and* "representation" of "emotion" possible, see C. Brodsky, "Whatever Moves You …," in *Traditions of Experiment from the Enlightenment to the Present. Essays in the Honor of Peter Demetz.* Ed. Nancy Kaiser and David E. Wellbery. Ann Arbor: University of Michigan, 1992, 17–43.

of the same name (*Paradoxe sur le comédien* [first pub. 1770 in *Correspondance littéraire*), this is the paradox of any acting subject— ultimately any subject, acting on any stage—who does, with sufficient practice, hone the experience of emotion into a language, but only on condition that he or she feel nothing. Commenting first that any French or English actor, whether literally or figuratively translating him or herself across the Channel to take part in a tragedy by Shakespeare or Racine, respectively, would be so "bound" ("enlacés") by their own disparate, culturally contingent understandings of the "same signs" ("mêmes signes") as to most resemble Laokoon and sons being squeezed to death by "serpents," Diderot observes further that indeed any two actors, or even any single actor who plays a role more than once, would suffer the same dismal fate.[11] For even when the "words" of their texts are composed with greatest "clarity," "precision" and "energy," these, like all "words, are only and can only be signs that approximate a thought, a feeling, an idea" ("les mots ne sont et ne peuvent être que des signes approchés d'une pensée, d'un sentiment, d'une idée"). Employing the same terms of Saussure's great insight one and a half centuries later, Diderot defines "signs" not as identities, with intrinsic—depictable and translatable—meaning, but as operative "values" within a self-defining, differential system, which, as such, must be "completed" within any specific dramatic context by the supplementary external means of "movement, gesture, tone, face, eyes, and given circumstance [of their speaker]" ("signes dont le mouvement, le geste, le ton, le visage, les yeux, la circonstance donnée complètent la valeur").[12] Just when you believe the actor to be most moved by "actual sentiment" ("le sentiment actuel"), "all his talent consists not in *feeling*, as you suppose, but in rendering so scrupulously the external signs of sentiment that you are deceived" ("tout son talent consiste non pas à *sentir*, comme vous le supposez, mais à rendre scrupuleusement les signes extérieures du sentiment, que vous vous y trompez."[13]). "Extreme sensibility makes for mediocre actors, mediocre sensibility makes for the multitude of bad actors" ("c'est l'extrême sensibilité qui fait les acteurs médiocres; c'est la sensibilité médiocre qui fait la multitude des mauvais acteurs"), but it is above all "the absolute absence of any sensibility that prepares sublime actors" ("c'est le manque absolu de sensibilité qui prépare les acteurs

11. Diderot, *Oeuvres*, XX: 46.
12. Ibid.
13. Diderot, *Oeuvres*, XX: 45 (emphasis added).

sublimes"), those who, compelled to externalize memory completely, rehearsing and repeating the signs they will perform "before a mirror" ("repéter ... devant une glace"), "naturally" reproduce the visible evidence of emotion most effectively.[14] *Their* tears, that so move *us,* "descend from the brain" ("descendent de son cerveau"), rather than "rise from the heart" ("montent du coeur"), and "were this not the case" ("s'il en était autrement ..."), "the condition of the actor" ("la condition du comédien"), practiced mimic of the "symptoms" of emotions, "would be the most unfortunate" ("serait la plus malheureuse des conditions"), and, one might add, the most improbable, since doomed to succeed in representing feelings by destroying the actual experience of feelings, which, when most "profound" ("profondes"), is expressed by no language but "mute" ("muets").[15]

A kind of playlet without plot whose two speakers ("the first" and "the second") play their opposing parts, of rational analyst and undiscerning sentimentalist, to the hilt, the *Paradox of the Actor* demonstrates Diderot's thesis precisely by mirroring it in a dialogue of simulated spontaneity in which the alternating absence and presence of a single exclamation mark across iterations of the "same sign" renders visible to the reader all that needs to be said about the theory of acting being enacted: in "the great actor," "the first" states matter-of-factly, there must be "a cold and tranquil spectator... and no sensibility" ("un spectateur froid et tranquille...et nulle sensibilité"); " "Nulle sensibilité!" exclaims the incredulous "second" in response; "Nulle" ("None"), "the first" reiterates categorically.[16]

The necessary separation between "sensibility" and expression ascribed in alternating expressions of incredulity and certainty to the successful performance here extends well beyond the enclosed space of the stage. Attributing the sacrifice of actual internal experience to the demands of and for representation within human interaction in general, Diderot's "first" ("cerebral") speaker turns the tables on his ("sensible" or "sensitive") "second" by training his spotlight of examination on his interlocutor directly, asking pointedly:

Is it at the moment you lose your friend or your mistress that you compose a poem on his or her death? No ... It is after the great pain

---

14. Diderot, *Oeuvres,* XX: 55.
15. Diderot, *Oeuvres,* XX: 56–57, 59.
16. Diderot, *Oeuvres,* XX: 48.

is past, when extreme feeling has atrophied, when one is far from the catastrophe, that the soul is calm, that one remembers one's eclipsed happiness, that one is capable of appreciating the loss one has undergone, and memory unites with imagination, the former to retrace, the latter to exaggerate the sweetness of a time now past, that one possesses oneself and *speaks well* ... one says one cries, but only because one is busy trying to render one's lines harmonious; otherwise, if tears flow, the pen falls from the hand.

[Est-ce au moment où vous venez de perdre votre ami ou votre maîtresse que vouz composerez un poème sur sa mort? Non ... C'est lorsque la grande douleur est passée, quand l'extrême sensibilité est amortie, lorsqu'on est loin de la catastrophe, que l'âme est calme, qu'on se rappelle son bonheur éclipsé, qu'on est capable d'apprécier la perte qu'on a faite, que la mémoire se réunit à l'imagination, l'une pour retracer, l'autre pour exagérer la douceur d'un temps passé; qu'on se possède et qu'on *parle bien* .... on dit qu'on pleure, mais on ne pleure pas lorsqu'on s'occupe à rendre son vers harmonieux: ou si les larmes coulent, la plume tombe de la main.[17]]

At the time of its linguistic expression, it is not feeling, but the mimetic memory of it, exaggerated by imagination, that enables now atrophied emotion to be composed and communicated in external form. The same holds true for any "you." Whether on the stage, in the street, in the boudoir, or "in" the brain, external forms of expression and experiences of emotion as strong as any Rousseau ascribes to the "savage man" may depart from an unreflective state of equilibrium, whose accompanying horizon of movement is so familiar as to go unnoticed, to enter, with Wordsworth's narrated subject, a "scene" without horizon in which familiar images appear emptied of content, and "forms" perceived to possess their own motive force pass "through" us without becoming "part" of us, "internalized," represented, known (nor even, in Kant's sense, abstractly predicated by a verbally enacted "power to judge"). In this the actor Diderot calls "sublime," in that he has no "inside" to be "lost" or "eclipsed," has a natural advantage over any "feeling" "actor"—whether of pre-scripted or specifically unscripted and thus aesthetically *and* ethically constitutive events—in that discontinuity already defines his every "horizon," his only "home." Never a subject of experience in the first place, the proficient actor comes

17. Diderot, *Oeuvres*, XX: 79.

closest to Rousseau's "natural man" in inhabiting a continuous void of "passion" or "feeling" unaffected by presence, absence, or event. Like Rousseau's "pre"-linguistic or potential "man" *before* the unprecedented intersubjective encounter and ensuing chain of events that, "after many experiences," allow him to recognize in another his own specular double, all is the same to the actor carrying no even latent internality "within" him; to him all means to the end (of reducing actual experience to the visible affect thereof) are good. And the imitative skill with which he learns to fill that void, repetitively calculating "before a mirror" how best to combine the visible "signs" observed and culled from others' "experiences," makes no difference whatsoever to, constitutes no experience for him. "One says," says Diderot's "first" speaker, "that actors have no character because in playing all they lose that which nature gave them, that they become false, as the doctor, the surgeon, the butcher become hard. I believe that one has taken the cause for the effect, and that they are only fit to play all, because they have none to begin with" ("On a dit que les comédiens n'avaient aucun caractère, parce qu'en les jouant tous ils perdaient celui que la nature leur avait donné, qu'ils devenaient faux, comme le médecin, le chirurgien et le boucher deviennent durs. Je crois qu'on a pris la cause pour l'effet, et qu'ils ne sont propres à les jouer tous que parce qu'ils n'en ont point."[18])

The subject most fit to compose a "language of emotion" is one in whom the external world never causes the experience of emotion, of irrational or incommensurate passion, in the first place. But this is so not because such an "actor" (in the ambiguous sense of agent or impersonator the word suggests) strives to control, regulate, and dissimulate such "involuntary movement," like the rest of us living and acting off the boards, but because he contains no "inside" whose movement could possibly come into conflict with any he encounters on the "outside," not even in the experience of ignorance and incomprehension of the empirical of which, as recounted in Rousseau's hypothetical narrative, and described in Kant's theory of judgment, passions and language are born. The actor–impersonator combines the external "signs" of others' emotion into a "language" just as he portrays human life in the form of observable characters, because neither immediate experiences of feeling nor internal proclivities of "character" get in "his" way.

Beyond and before its narrator's stated ambition to become a writer, during the research of the "lost" or deceased "time" of past experience

---

18. Diderot, *Oevures*, XX: 96–97.

that its narrator attempts to recover in writing, Proust's *Recherche* describes how our experience of experience, including the emotions that color experience or affect us, relate to representation in the first place. In the justly celebrated pages devoted to the kitchenmaid at Combray—unwitting victim, we discover later, of the externally indiscernible tortures inflicted upon her by Françoise, first-in-command in the kitchen who, even while requiring the presence of someone whose assistance she commands, refuses to allow the exercise of her sovereignty to be limited to any objectively given person—the narrator first describes "la fille de cuisine" not as a particular individual but a general concept: "a moral [or abstract]" rather than actual "person" whose "permanent institution" assured its "continuity and identity across the succession of passing forms in which it embodied itself " ("une personne morale, une institution permanente ... une sorte de continuité et d'identité, à travers la succession des formes passagères en lesquelles elle s'incarnait"[19]). The "institution[al]" concept of "the kitchenmaid" is first attached by the narrator to the perceptible reality of one particular kitchenmaid in the context of his recalling that Swann had taken to calling this otherwise anonymous embodiment in "a succession of passing forms" by the name of another "embodied" concept, that of one of the Virtues in Giotto's series of allegorical paintings in the Arena Chapel, of which Swann had given the narrator photographs.[20] Interconnected as casually as they are causally, the dizzying crossovers between abstract and concrete, or internally and externally based conceptions of "the kitchenmaid" in the narrative could be narrated, strictly sequentially, to unfold something like this: an *abstract* or "moral person" first *manifests itself as* a *concrete* or material person *in being named for* the *abstract* moral quality *allegorically* assigned to the *concrete* image (manifested by its photographic duplicate image) that—closing the circle—the real embodiment "resembles." Recollecting that this particular, visibly pregnant embodiment of the general conceptual abstraction we might entitle "Kitchenmaid" did "in effect resemble" ("ressemblait en effet") Giotto's rendering of a bodily person to represent the abstract concept of "Charity," the narrator manages to make the interrelation of the two concepts appear at once narrative and logical, like a palindrome turning upon the repetition of a shared externality, one concept's temporary, human embodiment mirroring the fixed, allegorical embodiment of another. Yet the narrator

19. Proust, *A la recherche*, I: 80.
20. Ibid.

compounds that purely metonymically induced identification of the one figure with the other by the characteristically "ironic"[21] Swann by proceeding to state that Giotto's "Charity" and the current iteration of "Kitchenmaid" also resemble each other when considered intellectually, and, as it turns out, negatively, for both the real woman present in the kitchen and the reproducible image of a woman in Giotto's allegorical painting do not convey in any sense whatsoever the idea they are supposed to symbolize:

> I realize now that these Virtues and Vices of Padua resembled [the kitchenmaid] in yet another manner. In the same way that the image of this girl was augmented by the added symbol that she carried before her stomach without appearing to comprehend its meaning, without there being anything in her face that translated the beauty and the spirit of that sense—as if it were simply a heavy load—so it is without any apparent suspicion of what she is about that the powerful housewife who is represented in the Arena Chapel beneath the name "Charity" ... embodies this virtue ... without any thought of charity seeming to have ever been able to be expressed by this energetic and vulgar face.

> [Et je me rends compte maintenant que ces Vertus et ces Vices de Padoue lui ressemblaient encore d'une autre manière. De même que l'image de cette fille était accrue par le symbole ajouté qu'elle portait devant son ventre, sans avoir l'air d'en comprendre le sens, sans que rien dans son visage en traduisit la beauté et l'esprit, comme un

---

21. Proust, *A la recherche,* I: 97–98. In appearing not only conscious of but committed to the superficiality of the culturally incongruous comparison (between a canonical image of high "culture" and a visibly beleaguered day laborer) upon which his nickname for the "kitchenmaid" draws, Swann is speaking with the same "ironic tone" soon to be remarked upon in the narrative, by which he both indicates and conceals whatever it is he "seriously thinks" "in face of things." I have analyzed the direct relation of Swann's "ironic" mode of speech, and the hermeneutic curiosity it awakens in the narrator, to the narrator's own concealed invention of the detailed third-person narrative, "Un Amour de Swann," and the entirety of the first-person narrative spun of comparisons made on the model of Swann's that succeeds it, in "Remembering Swann," *Imposition of Form, op. cit.,* pp. 262–306, abridged and collected in the Norton Critical Edition of *Swann's Way.* Ed. Susanna Lee (New York: Norton, 2014, pp. 470–492).

simple et pesant fardeau, de même c'est sans paraître s'en douter que la puissante ménagère qui est représentée à l'Arena au-dessous du nom 'Caritas' … incarne cette vertu… sans qu'aucune pensée de charité semble avoir jamais pu être exprimée par son visage énergique et vulgaire.[22]]

Such, says the narrator, is the defining characteristic of all Giotto's allegorical portraits: their negation of, or at very least distraction from, the very vice or virtue they are stated to represent. For these are specifically pictoral allegories—pictures of objects meant to indicate something "other" (*allius*) than the specificity of those objects themselves—and, as such, they must fail to unite presence with representation. The unceremonious rendering of physicality in Giotto's allegorical action figures—a hand "'passing'" "a heart" "to God" "as a cook passes a corkscrew"; "feet trampling the treasures of the earth… as [one] stamps grapes to extract juice or rather climbs on sacks to gain height" ("Charity"); "a snake filling a wide-open mouth" to the point of its "distortion," "like that of a child inflating a balloon with his breath" ("Envy")—fixes our "attention" with such "concentrat[ion]" as to "scarcely leave time" for "thoughts" for the concepts by which they are entitled, and, even though Swann "professed to admire them," the narrator admits that, at the time, he could not understand why.[23] Only "later" ("plus tard'), he states, did he understand the "arresting strangeness, the special beauty of these frescoes," which

had to do with the great place that the symbol occupied in them, and the fact that it was represented not as a symbol, since the symbolized thought was not expressed, but as real, as effectively undergone or materially handled, gave to the meaning of the work something more literal and precise … These Vices and Virtues of Padua must have had a great deal of reality in them because they appeared to me as

22. Proust, *A la recherche*, I: 81: "elle… 'passe'" "à Dieu" "son cœur" "comme une cuisinière passe un tire-bouchon"; "elle foule aux pieds les trésors de la terre, … comme si elle piétinait des raisins pour en extraire le jus ou plutôt comme elle aurait monté sur des sacs pour se hausser"; "le serpent qui siffle aux lèvres … remplit si complètement sa bouche grande ouverte … que les muscles de sa figure sont détendus pour pouvoir le contenir, comme ceux d'un enfant qui gonfle un ballon."
23. Ibid.

living as the pregnant servant, and she herself didn't seem to me much less allegorical [than them]. And perhaps this, at least apparent non-participation of the soul of a being in the virtue that acts through it, has apart from its aesthetic value a reality that, while not psychological is at least, as one says, physiognomic. When, later, I had occasion to meet in the course of my life, in convents, for example, truly sainted incarnations of charity in action, they generally had the cheerful, positive, indifferent and brusque air of a busy surgeon, that visage in which one reads no commiseration, no tenderness before human suffering, no fear of colliding with it, and which is the face without sweetness, the antipathetic and sublime face of true goodness.

[Mais plus tard, j'ai compris que l'étrangeté saisissante, la beauté spéciale de ces fresques tenait à la grande place que le symbole y occupait, et que le fait qu'il fût représenté non comme un symbole puisque la pensée symbolique n'était pas exprimée, mais comme réel, comme effectivement subi ou matériellement manié, donnait à la signification de l'oeuvre quelque chose de plus littéral et plus précis . . . Il fallait que ces Vertus et ces Vices de Padoue eussent en eux bien de la réalité puisqu'ils m'apparaissaient comme aussi vivants que la servante enceinte, et qu'elle-même ne me semblait pas beaucoup moins allégorique. Et peut-être cette non-participation, du moins apparente, de l'âme d'un être à la vertu qui agit par lui, a aussi en dehors de sa valeur esthétique une réalité sinon psychologique, au moins, comme on dit, physiognomonique. Quand, plus tard, j'ai eu l'occasion de rencontrer au cours de ma vie, dans des couvents par exemple, des incarnations vraiment saintes de la charité active, elles avaient généralement un air allègre, positif, indifférent et brusque de chirurgien pressé, ce visage où ne se lit aucune commisération, aucun attendrissement devant la souffrance humaine, aucune crainte de la heurter, et qui est le visage sans douceur, le visage antipathique et sublime de la vraie bonté.[24]]

This circuit of mimetic miscues—of an apparently obliviously pregnant kitchenmaid who looks like an allegorical figure who looks nothing like an allegory but rather like a kitchenmaid who carries her pregnancy before and apart from her, like a physical load—is based in the *non*symbolic quality of the symbol, its failure either to represent or suggest the sense of what it is supposed to signify and unintended

24. Proust, *A la recherche*, I: 82 (emphasis added).

similarity to a specifically "passing form" of the most neglected of domestic figures instead. As described by Proust's narrator, Giotto's "materially handled" figures appear as coldly "indifferent" to the "symbolic" content of their actions as do "the truly saintly incarnations of active charity" he has "encountered in the course of his life." Such foregrounding of "material" over conceptual qualities may have a certain "aesthetic value" and a "reality" "we call physiognomic," but, in that it leaves the "psychological" quite out of the picture, this physiognomy without psychology would be more like a death mask than an expression of "active" life. It is indeed of "the thinking of the dying" ("la pensée des agonisants") that these nonsymbolic symbols make the narrator think next, a "thinking" he describes as "turned toward the effective, the painful, the visceral underside" of their experience: an experience of the "materially" effective "underside of death which is precisely the side that it presents to them . . . and that more closely resembles that of a load that crushes them . . . than that which we call the idea of death" ("tournée vers le côté effectif, douloureux, viscéral, vers cet envers de la mort qui est précisément le côté qu'elle leur présente . . . et qui ressemble beaucoup plus à un fardeau qui les écrase . . . qu'à ce que nous appelons l'idée da la mort"[25]).

Our nonsymbolic perception of the bodies of symbols that have been "materially" rather than conceptually "handled" reminds the narrator of the nonsymbolic experience of any body whose "thinking" is "turned"—in the "agonizing" consciousness of itself being "materially handled" by, itself "submitted" to its own dying—to the "effective" rather than ideational "side . . . of death." Like the opacity of Giotto's allegories, his "Charity without charity,"[26] that "effective side" remains outside our minds, impervious to whatever else we might think: not expressive but inexpressive, an immutable and intellectually intransmutable weight. In this Proust's visibly nonsymbolic symbol and its internal equivalent, "thinking" experienced as the bearing of a "crushing load," perfectly describe, in narrative, mimetic terms, the "actual" ("eigentliche") experience of the "symbol" theorized in Hegel's *Aesthetics*. For Hegel, as for no philosopher before or after him, the aesthetic is, explicitly, the origin of philosophy,[27] and the aesthetic

25. Ibid.

26. Proust, *A la recherche*, I: 81.

27. G. W. F. Hegel, *Vorlesungen über die Ästhetik*, Bd. 13, in *Werke*, 20 Bde., Hrsg. Eva Moldernhauer and Karl Markus Michel (Frankfurt: Suhrkamp, 1986), XIII: 139.

originates,[28] just as explicitly, *not* with "beauty," viewed as either ideal concept or object, but rather the encounter with a specific *semantic* problem: the encounter with what Hegel calls the "essential *ambiguity* of the symbol."[29] The inherent semantic "ambiguity" of any effective "symbol," no matter how august or trivial, for Hegel, is identical to that of every Duchesse and Kitchenmaid, "phrase" and extended narration, "jeune fille" and "fleur," nominal and concrete object Proust's narrator represents in the differentiating act of its recollection: every word uttered, as if "between quotation marks," by his infinitely enigmatic Swann, no less than every physical detail in each misleadingly personified Virtue Giotto paints. It is the ambiguity that asks the question, am I hiding what I mean to say or openly indicating what I am systematically meant to say; am I a "symbol" or a "sign"? For as soon as a specific "meaning" is assigned a "symbol," i.e., as soon as a "symbol" is understood to stand, unambiguously, for something else, it reverts or devolves into what it was "in the first place" a purely, i.e., "merely arbitrary," denotative "sign,"[30] whose similarly infinite variety of material forms and assigned meanings across and within "the differentiation of languages" ("die Verscheidenheit der Sprachen"[31]) owes to the fact that, in itself, any sign, *as* sign, can be attached to any meaning at all.

28. Hegel, *Vorlesungen,* XIII: 393: "The symbol, in the meaning of the word we use here, constitutes the beginning of art, both conceptually and as an historical appearance" ("Das Symbol in der Bedeutung in welcher wir das Wort hier gebrauchen, macht dem Begriff wie der historischen Erscheinung nach dem Anfang der Kunst").

29. After demonstrating that, since a "symbol," by definition, never signifies what it indicates, an "infinite number of existences and formations" ("unendlich vielen Existenzen und Gestaltungen") may be used either to convey or *not* to convey "symbolic" meaning, Hegel writes: "From this it follows that, according to its own conception, the symbol remains essentially *ambiguous*" ("Hieraus folgt nun, dass das Symbol seinem eigenen Begriff nach wesentlich *zweideutig* bleibt" [Ibid., XIII: 396–397 emphasis in text]).

30. Hegel, *Vorlesungen,* Ibid., XIII: 357: "1. Now, the symbol is, in the first place, a *sign*. In mere denotation, however, the association that the meaning and its expression have with one another is only a completely arbitrary one." ("1. Das Symbol ist nun zunächst ein *Zeichen*. Bei der blossen Bezeichnung aber ist der Zusammenhang, den die Bedeutung und deren Ausdruck miteinander haben, nur eine ganz willkürliche Verknüpfung." [emphasis in text])

31. Hegel, *Vorlesungen,* XIII: 394.

In order to remain "permanently ambiguous," the meaning of any "symbol" must be the question: do I conceal meaning? The "monstrous crystals" ("ungeheure Kristalle"[32]) that are the "symbols" in which the aesthetic originates in the *Aesthetics* openly hide embalmed bodies from view. In the "pyramids" of the Egyptians material content is preserved forever by, and in separation from material form, and, with the building of those geometrically perfected enclosures above ground and excavation of impenetrable labyrinths beneath them, the unknowable dead can be known only to be—and thus for the first time known really to be—dead, i.e., removed from all actual interaction, materially or intellectually changeable into nothing else. Embodying for the first time "the fixed distinction of the living from the dead *as* dead" ("die feste Unterscheidung des Lebendigen von den Toten *als* Toten"[33] [emphasis added]), these "housings of the dead" ("Behausungen für Toten"[34]) remain just as unenlightened by the "hieroglyphs" that cover their surfaces as do the bodies permanently concealed within their sealed forms, "riddles" made to remain "indecipherable," then as now.[35] Whatever the specific historical and cultural truth value of what Hegel thought when his "thinking" "turned toward" the opaque, "effective" "side" that is, exactly, every "side" of the pyramids, and whatever we may think of his understanding of the pyramids and the symbol now, no less than a pregnancy carried like a "heavy load" by a titular Kitchenmaid, or the "crush[ing]" "weight" that is the "underside" of any body rendered alien to consciousness by dying, they, too, represent the

32. Hegel, *Vorlesungen*, XIII: 459.

33. Hegel, *Vorlesungen*, XIV: 291.

34. Ibid.

35. "But the Egyptian symbols [and hieroglyphics] …contain much implicitly, not explicitly. These are works undertaken in the attempt to become clear about oneself, but during this struggle for meaning in and of itself, they remain, nonetheless, at a standstill. In this sense we perceive in Egyptian artworks that they contain riddles, whose correct decipherment not only we, in part, cannot reach but which, for the most part, cannot be reached by those who posed them for themselves." ("Aber die ägyptischen Symbole enthalten … implizit viel, explicit nicht. Es sind Arbeiten, mit dem Versuche unternommen, sich selber klarzuwerden, doch sie bleiben bei dem Ringen an und für sich Deutlichen stehen. In diesem Sinne sehen wir es die ägyptischen Kunstwerke an, das sie Rätsel enthalten, für welche zum Teil nicht nur uns, sondern am meisten denen, die sie sich selber aufgaben, die rechte Entzifferung nicht gelingt.") (Hegel, *Vorlesungen*, XIII: 465).

impersonal "burden," or "fardeau,"[36] unifying the opaque side of all things, matter that, housing more matter, blocks all "enlightening" entry into or intellectual lightening of its "load." Yet, like Rousseau's similarly necessarily speculative narrative of the "origin" of language in the encounter with corporeal otherness, the experience of impenetrable and "indecipherable" sensory distinctness that Hegel ascribes to the material "symbol" is also, on his account, the origin of the mind *as* mind, capable of differing in thought from the body of which it is a part, and thus also of shaping matter into the means through which it acts and reflects, *and* recognizing, critically if intermittently, therein, the "real" incommensurability of all delimited means to the capacity to experience, produce, and reflect upon difference that they express.[37]

For Hegel as for Proust, such incommensurability does not stand for a depth of "interiority" but a real and permanent ignorance of the hidden workings or reason of the "materially different" (to use Wordsworth's words), opaque "riddles" one perceives, whether these appear to betoken the animating "virtue" *or* actual "death" of the same. "This at least apparent non-participation of the soul of a being in the virtue that acts through it," which is to say, the visibly non-mimetic, or inapparent relation between the being we see and the active contents it represents, "call" it "allegory," "hieroglyph," "pyramid," or merely "a heavy load," are "symbols" without entry points whose contents remain contents for that very reason, different from the open, undifferentiating light of day. What one sees may be a particular embodiment of the abstract idea that embodiment occludes—"Kitchenmaid" or "Charity" or "Envy"—or it may be "housings of the dead" built to remove their bodily contents forever from view, matter containing matter that remains material in being made invisible ("unsichtbar"[38]), and so physically and intellectually untranslatable, inaccessible to being emoted, moved outside from within. Conversely, at the other end of the spectrum of experience narrated by Rousseau, what one "sees" may be the displacement of an emotion upon an object, the mistaken projection

36. See n. 22, n. 25, this Chapter.

37. I have treated Hegel's analysis of the symbol in greater detail in: "From the Pyramids to Romantic Poetry: Housing the Spirit in Hegel," in *Rereading Romanticism*, ed. Martha Helfer (Amsterdam: Rodopi, 2000), pp. 327–366; "Szondi and Hegel: 'The Troubled Relationship of Literary Criticism to Philosophy," *Telos.* Special Issue on Peter Szondi and Critical Hermeneutics, No 140 (2007): 45–64.

38. Hegel, *Vorlesungen*, XIII: 460.

of a passion, brought to life by empirical ignorance, upon the empirical, subsequently corrected, on the basis of "many" empirical "experiences," by its division into two externally comparable objects, and so buried, by the very language it occasions, ever more thoroughly from view.

In reality—as Proust's narrator describes *after* describing the "reality" of *non*symbolic symbols—people appear to us, for the most part, just like pyramids: "A real being, no matter how deeply we sympathize with him, remains, for the most part, perceived by our senses, which is to say, he remains opaque, offers a dead weight that our sensibility cannot raise" ("Un être réel, si profondément que nous sympathisions avec lui, pour une grande part est perçu par nos sens, c'est-à-dire nous reste opaque, offre un poids mort que notre sensibilité ne peut soulever[39]). "The discovery of the novelist," the narrator continues,

> was to have the idea of replacing these impenetrable parts of the soul with an equal quantity of immaterial parts, that is to say, those that our soul can assimilate. What does it matter that, from then on, the actions, the emotions of these beings of a new genre appear to us as true, since we have made them ours, since it is in us that they are produced ... in a state, where, as in all purely interior states, all emotion is decoupled.
>
> [La trouvaille du romancier a été d'avoir l'idée de remplacer ces parties impénétrables à l'âme par une quantité égale de parties immatérielles, c'est-à-dire que notre âme peut s'assimiler. Qu'importe dès lors que les actions, les émotions de ces êtres d'un nouveau genre nous apparaissent comme vraies, puisque nous les avons faites nôtres, puisque c'est en nous qu'elles se produisent ... dans cet état, où comme dans tous les états purement intérieurs toute émotion est décuplée.[40]]

Proust's narrator, then, extends to people Hegel's notion of the "essentially ambiguous," impenetrable "real being" of the symbol even while praising pure fiction, inverting Diderot's model of externally effective and internally vacuous representation by endorsing the notion of a full, but entirely fictive interiority, one which "decouples" the "immaterial" "emotions" it produces, as replacement for a reality it cannot assimilate, from any connection whatsoever to the real it perceives outside it. This may well be the view held by Proust's narrator,

39. Proust, *A la recherche*, I: 85.
40. Ibid.

self-described novelist-in-the-making, of the pleasures of "states" that are "purely interior," as limitless and deathless as pure fiction, "immaterial." Yet this is the same narrator who describes the intellectual impasse he experiences when encountering the "irony" with which Swann speaks his mind as if it were not his mind; his bafflement before the reproductions of "allegorical" paintings lent him by Swann that, failing to suggest the titular Virtues they are meant to represent, are employed by Swann as tropes for real people they recall in only the most materially expressive, external sense; and his own conception of "the visceral underside … of death" that, bearing no resemblance to "what we call the idea of death," is experienced by the dying like a conceptually inalleviable, "materially" "crushing load," a fully alien body to whose insuperable "effect" they are compelled to "turn [their] thought." Encompassing at once both these observations of the actual experience of an irreducible exteriority and the power of the "novelist" to replace just such material opacities with fiction, the narrator then proceeds to provide his reader with a view of something no subject can experience and whose replacement no novelist can invent.

The narrator calls this "the real horizon," in which not only the "production" of fictive "emotions" and "actions" from stored external perceptions and "reflection[s] that our soul has projected upon them"—a transformation that, capable of exceeding all known experience and phenomenal limits, is now defined, in a further "decoupling" from the real, as the "simple association" of things with "ideas" derived not from things but from books—but even the very movement of consciousness, of "inside to outside," is "enveloped": "Finally, in continuing to follow from the inside to the outside the simultaneously juxtaposed states in my consciousness, and before arriving at *the real horizon* that enveloped them, I found pleasures of another genre … " ("Enfin, en continuant à suivre du dedans au dehors les états simultanément juxtaposés dans ma conscience, et avant d'arriver jusqu'à l'horizon réel qui les enveloppait, je trouve des plaisirs d'un autre genre …"[41]). These latter are the habitual sensory "pleasures" provided to him empirically by life in Combray, and it is to these that the narrator next turns his attention in loving detail, leaving the enigmatic "real horizon" extending in every direction, so as to "envelop" all conscious and emotive "states" we produce internally, unreached. Unlike Wordsworth's optical horizon, a purely visual delineation imposed by the situational act of looking outward from one's position on the enveloping curvature of the earth, this

---

41. Proust, *A la recherche*, I: 87 (emphasis added).

horizon is not an ever-shifting source of self-orientation, a sensory limit
that, contrary to the conceptual limit posed by the "essential ambiguity"
of the pyramid, has no actual independence from its viewer and so
cannot help but permit itself to be traversed. It is, instead, impossibly,
called "real," that is, not the product of either internal emotion and
tropological projection or fleeting sense perception alone.

There can be, of course, no such "real horizon" in reality insofar as we
see and experience reality. Yet it is something *in effect* like those
pyramids, "husks" ("Hülle"[42]) that could well be called the "real horizon"
both with regard to the bodies that will never see out of them and the
living who will never see inside them, "real being[s]" whose "unknown
modes of being" we cannot assimilate or integrate into ourselves: "huge
and mighty forms" or a "vulgar" embodiment of "charity"; "others" like
us who appear nothing like us because we've never seen either our
"others" or ourselves before; or another who appears to "act" just like us
precisely because, when not performing that resemblance, he is nothing
like us at all. With good reason, Paul de Man distrusted both all talk of
emotion and all inside/outside metaphors, viewing them, as Diderot or
Rousseau might say, as taking the effect for the cause, and thereby
removing us ever further from the "real beings," of actual, historical
effectivity, designated by the terms they loosely conjoin ("talk" and
"emotion," "inside" and "outside," things "that do not live like living men"
and the "mises en scène" of our interactions with them in literature).
Perhaps that is why, in his writing on Proust, he analyzes the narrator's
figural use of these, his talking of emotion as of a passing from outside
to inside and back again, as between person and painting, and material
opacity and "fiction," *without* mentioning the narrator's own indication
of "the real horizon" apart from and "envelop[ping]" all such figures,
especially in his descriptions of the act of reading. For, as an experience
of language as such, necessarily unlimited, in its radically abstract
enactment, by personal, environmental, or any other "external" factors,
the reading or intellectual reception of language is perhaps the only
experience we both undergo and enact whose antecedent object or
"outside" (i.e., any concrete sign operative within a system of signs) is,
by definition, *external and material yet also abstract* in its very existence,
and whose subject or "inside" is, by equal definition, *internal and
intellectual, yet also illustrative,* or *referential* (i.e., "external") in the
composition of its "content," i.e., its very particular, because virtually
unlimited effect.

42. Hegel, *Vorlesungen*, XIV: 292.

If ever one could really "think," let alone "rethink emotion" (not to speak of the necessarily "figural," because fundamentally chiastic, "inside" and "outside" crossing activity of "reading") without committing an act of oxymoron misrepresenting both, it would have to be from the very line of "the real horizon" Proust's narrator names but does not reach, which is to say, from the position without horizon of a body without "involuntary motions," not "subject" to the temporal experience of *any* sensory and intellectual differentiation, and thus without decipherable signs or tells of any kind. Like Proust, de Man did not go "there," that is, commit to the empty figural conceit and additionally falsifying false step of talking about this place where inside and outside, and the language that denotes them, really no longer prevail. For this would be a "real" devoid of any conception of the real, of agency or authorship of any kind: "where" *every* "visible scene would enter unawares into [the] mind," no "thing could feel the touch of earthly years," and so no "Lucy" (or any other "worthy purpose") could ever even be designated let alone aimed toward, and the earth-bound difference between "darkness and the light" that we "incompeten[tly]" "call" "Imagination," never experienced as an unearthly conflict, a moon abruptly "dropp'd" from sight, or any unanticipated, inherently consequential event, indeed ever be perceived *to occur* at all.

Yet like Proust also, de Man knew a false horizon, a bad metaphor, when he saw one, and that any indication of "the real horizon," unlike these, delimits a *critical* position without bodily position. "Real" because neither purely optically nor intellectually projected, the limit that is the "self"-critical condition produced by the activity of thinking we call "critical" is a standing capacity not to "be" (whatever that might be) but *to represent*, and thereby differentiate "oneself" from any particular, empirically defined position. The "true difficulty" separating "knowledge" from "power" in Wordsworth, and the limit entailing the pivotal "power to judge" in Kant,[43] it stands for the difference *between* thinking and

43. See *The Linguistic Condition,* "Preface," on "standing a chance," esp.; Part I, Chap. 1 and Chap. 2, Sec. 1–8; Chap. 2, Sec. 11, on Wordsworth in particular; and Part II, Chap. 3, Sec. 1, *et passim,* on the limit position of the "power to judge" between cognition and moral action in Kant, i.e., Kant's definition of the "field" in which that power to judge is exercised purely in function of its negative delimitation of these other capacities, in that judgment, he specifies, disposes of "no field of objects as its own realm" ("kein Feld der Gegenstände als sein Gebiet zuständе" [Kant, *KU,* B XXII–XXIII, X: 85])

emotion, "action" and "reaction," "subject" and "every other," and "word" and "object," as between a recognizably symbolized (or, for that matter, putatively pure) "idea," and the vital, "essential ambiguity of the symbol" dividing "the dead" *from* "the living," in Hegel. Never capable of completing itself in the mode of a perfected geometrical figure, that critical limit instead delineates, with all the clarity of apparent "indifference," the occasion for unprecedented action that both Kant and Hegel call "aesthetic."

For, just as the "feeling of freedom" "felt" before an unknown object frees any subject to turn outside itself, to exchange "his" or "her" "I" for that of "every other" in the act of *speaking* the "power to judge" in a "general voice" according to Kant,[44] or, in Wordsworth's terms, to "consider man and the objects that surround him as acting and re-acting upon each other," doing "what the Poet does" in "the language really used by men," so Hegel's "actual symbolic"—double origin of aesthetic experience *and* philosophy alike—relates the material and semiotic dimensions at work within every linguistic formation into a free-"standing" "riddle" of meaning[45] posed at any time of anyone. Shorn of visible "horizon," the deictically independent field of action that both Kant and Hegel describe is instead delimited by the interactions constituting the content of "real language." Enacted in "words" worthy of the name in that, unlike a necessarily codified "language of emotions," or fixed "symbols of the passions," they operate instead "as *things*, active and efficient, which are themselves part of the passion,"[46] "real language" enables the "tru[ly] difficult" passage from "power *to* knowledge,"[47] or activity to history, whose common "purpose" the poet identifies as the only "worthy" aim of poetry itself.

44. See *The Linguistic Condition*, Chap. 2: "The Condition of Judgment," Sec. 3, 4, 5, esp.

45. Hegel, *Vorlesungen*, XIII: 465: "In this sense, we perceive in Egyptian artworks that they contain riddles whose correct solution not only we, in part, cannot reach, but which, for the most part, cannot be reached by those themselves who posed them for themselves" ("In diesem Sinn sehen wir an den ägyptischen Kunstwerke an, dass sie Rätsel enthalten, für welche zum Teil nicht nur uns, sondern am meisten denen, die sich selber aufgaben, die rechte Entzifferung nicht gelingt").

46. See this study, Part I, Chap. 2, n. 4.

47. Ibid., Part I, Chap. 5 (n. 5).

In the sense that any horizon is merely, in Proust's words, the "passing form" of a concept, one "kitchenmaid" in a series of ephemeral appearances before a permanent and inscrutable arbiter—whether a "faculty of judgment" whose essential "condition" of "communicability" remains, in Kant's words, outside the realm of "research"; "the lost time" whose "research" remains intertwined with lived time; or an implacable power to transform raw into delectable material, "Françoise"— the "real horizon" we enact in language and can never see, let alone reach, may instead define the purview of some "unknown mode of being," perhaps that "real being" which, "[f]or so it seemed, with purpose of its own/And measured motion, like a living thing/Str[i]de[s] after" our every purposeful action, too. Necessarily represented *a posteriori*, which is to say, "by sad incompetence of human speech," that same apparently purposeful "Power" we also "call" "Imagination" might well be called history: the unpredictable afterlife of actions whose "real horizon" we can neither perceive nor know, but, doing what Kant called "seeing as the poets do,"[48] "judge."

Any "real horizon" to speak of, as far as Kant can "see," would look less like an identifiable phenomenon we may perceive and represent than the ground of representation beneath our feet, the "common" verbal "ground" on which the critical, "free" act of judgment, in his words, "really" depends.[49] So for Wordsworth the only poetic language worthy of the name cannot be that which appears "poetic" from within a known linguistic field, its delimiting horizon as unreal in "being" as any we may see at any time, but the "language" we make "real," not phenomenally but "materially different," by our unpredictably— phenomenally unforeseeable—consequential interaction with it: "the language really used by men."

48. See Chap. 9, n. 26, this study; Kant, *KU* B 118–19, X:196. For an analysis of the unparalleled position granted poetry in the Third Critique and relation of the "Transcendental Aesthetics" of the First Critique to poetics, see *The Linguistic Condition*, Chap. 3, Sec. 3: "The Schema and the Language of Poetry," esp.

49. Kant, *KU*, B 68, X: 159. See *The Linguistic Condition*, Chap. 2, Sec. 1.

Bibliography

Primary Bibliography

Benjamin, Walter. *Illuminationen.* Hrsg. Siegfried Unseld. Frankfurt: Suhrkamp, 1977.

Diderot, Denis. *Oeuvres complètes,* 25 vols. Ed. H. Dieckmann, J. Fabre, J. Varloot, J Proust. Paris: Hermann, 1975–.

Edmund Husserl, *Husserliana,* 42— Bde. Versch. Hrsg. The Hague: Martinus Nijhoff, 1973–.

Hegel, G. W. F. *Theorie-Werkausgabe.* XX Bde. Hrsg. E. Moldenhauer and K. M. Michel. Frankfurt: Suhrkamp, 1969–71.

Kant, Immanuel. *Werkausgabe.* XII Bde. Hsrg. Wilhelm Weischedel. Frankfurt: Suhrkamp, 1974.

Kleist, Heinrich von. *Sämtliche Werke und Briefe.* 2 Bde. Hrsg. Helmut Sembdner. München: Deutscher Taschenbuch Verlag, 1987.

Lukács, Georg. *Die Theorie des Romans,* Berlin: Cassirer, 1920.

Proust, Marcel. *A la recherche du temps perdu.* 3 vols. Paris: Bibliothèque de la Pléiade, 1954.

Rousseau, Jean-Jacques. *Discours sur les sciences et les arts; Discours sur l'origine et les fondements de l'inégalité parmi les hommes.* Paris: Flammarion, 1992 [orig. pub. 1751; 1755].

Rousseau, Jean-Jacques. *Du contrat social ou Principes de droits politiques.* Paris: Flammarion, 1966 [orig. pub. 1762]

Rousseau, Jean-Jacques. *Essai sur l'origine des langues, où il est parlé de la mélodie et de l'imitation musicale.* Ed. Charles Porset. Paris: Nizet, 1969 [orig. pub. 1781; written 1740s?, 1750s?].

Rousseau, Jean-Jacques. *Essai sur l'origine des langues, où il est parlé de la mélodie et de l'imitation musicale.* Ed. Jean Starobinski. Paris: Gallimard, 1990.

Rousseau, Jean-Jacques. *Lettre à M. d'Alembert sur son article "Genève."* Ed. Michel Launay. Paris: Flammarion, 1967 [orig. pub. 1757].

de Saussure, Ferdinand. *Cours de linguistique générale.* Ed. Charles Bally, Albert Sechehaye, Albert Riedlinger. Paris: Payot, 1971 [orig. pub. 1916].

de Saussure, Ferdinand. *Cours de linguistique générale.* Rev. Edn, Ed. de Mauro. Paris: Payot, 1978.

Wordsworth, William. *The Fourteen-Book Prelude.* Ed. W. J. B. Owen. Ithaca: Cornell University Press, 1985 [orig. pub. 1805, 1850].

Wordsworth, William. *Lyrical Ballads and Other Poems, 1797–1800.* Ed. James Butler and Karen Green. Ithaca; Cornell University Press, 1992.

Wordsworth, William. *The Prose Works.* Ed. W. J. B. Owen and Jane Worthington Smyser. 2 vols. Oxford: Clarendon, 1974.

Wordsworth, William. *The Thirteen-Book Prelude.* Ed. Mark L. Reed. Ithaca: Cornell University Press, 1990.

Secondary Bibliography

Aarsleff, Hans. *From Locke to Saussure. Essays on the Study of Language and Intellectual History.* Minneapolis: University of Minnesota Press, 1982.

Barstow, Marjorie Latta. *Wordsworth's Theory of Poetic Diction.* New Haven: Yale University Press, 1917.

Barthes, Roland. *Mythologies.* Paris: Editions du Seuil, 1957.

Blanchot, Maurice. *L'espace littéraire.* Paris: Gallimard, 1954.

Brodsky, Claudia. "'A now not *toto caelo* a not now:' Husserl and the 'Origin' of Difference, from Number to Literature." In *Phenomenology to the Letter. Husserl and Literature.* Ed. Philippe Haensler and Rochelle Tobias. Berlin: de Gruyter, 2020, 1–31.

Brodsky, Claudia. "From the Pyramids to Romantic Poetry. Housing the Spirit in Hegel." In *Rereading Romanticism.* Ed. Martha Heller. Amsterdam: Rodopi, 1999, 327–66.

Brodsky, Claudia. *The Imposition of Form. Studies in Narrative Representation and Knowledge.* Princeton: Princeton University Press, 1987.

Brodsky, Claudia. *The Linguistic Condition. Kant's Critique of Judgment and the Poetics of Action.* London: Bloomsbury (forthcoming, 2020).

Brodsky, Claudia. "The Poetic Structure of Complexity: Wordsworth's Sublime and 'Something Regular,'" solicited contribution to *Wordsworth's Poetic Theory*, Ed. Stefan Hoesel-Uhlig and Alexander Regier. London: Palgrave, 2010, 81–102.

Brodsky, Claudia. "Remembering Swann." In *Swann's Way.* Norton Critical Edition. Ed. Susanna Lee. New York: Norton, 2014, 470–92.

Brodsky, Claudia. "Szondi and Hegel. 'The Troubled Relationship of Literary Criticism to Philosophy." *Telos.* no. 146 (2007): 45–64.

Brodsky, Claudia. "Whatever Moves You. 'Experimental Philosophy' and the Literature of Experience in Diderot and Kleist." In *Traditions of Experiment from the Enlightenment to the Present. Essays in the Honor of Peter Demetz.* Ed. Nancy Kaiser and David E. Wellbery. Ann Arbor: University of Michigan, 1992, 17–43.

Bromwich, David. *Disowned by Memory. Wordsworth's Poetry.* Chicago: University of Chicago Press, 1998.

Campbell, Sally Howard. *Rousseau and the Paradox of Alienation.* Plymouth, UK: Lexington Books, 2012.

Campe, Rüdiger. "Presenting the Affect: The Scene of Pathos in Aristotle's Rhetoric and its Revision in Descartes' *Passions of the Soul.*" In R. Campe and Julia Weber, eds, *Rethinking Emotion* (Berlin: de Gruyter, 2015), pp. 37–6.

Caraher, Brian G. *Wordsworth's "Slumber" and the Problematics of Reading.* University Park, Pa.: Pennsylvania State University Press, 1991.

Carter, Christiane Jane. *Rousseau and the Problem of War.* New York: Garland Press, 1987.

Cascardi, Anthony. *Consequences of Enlightenment.* Cambridge: Cambridge University Press, 1998).

Chandler, James. *Wordsworth's Second Nature: A Study of the Poetry and Politics.* Chicago: University of Chicago, 1984.

Clarke, C. C. *Romantic Paradox. An Essay on the Poetry of Wordsworth.* London: Routledge & Kegan Paul, 1962.

Crawford, David. *Kant's Aesthetic Theory.* Madison: University of Wisconsin, 1974.

Danby, John. *The Simple Wordsworth.* London: Routledge & Kegan Paul, 1971 [orig. pub. 1960].

Darbishire, Helen. *The Poet Wordsworth.* Oxford: Clarendon Press, 1950.

de Man, Paul. *Blindness and Insight.* Minneapolis: University of Minnesota Press, 1983 [orig. pub. 1971].

de Man, Paul. "The Temptation of Permanence." In *Critical Writings. 1953–1978.* Trans. Dan Latimer, ed. Lindsay Waters. Minneapolis: University of Minnesota Press, 1989 [orig. French pub. *Monde Nouveau*, Oct. 1955], 30–40.

Derrida, Jacques. *Marges de la philosophie.* Paris: Editions de Minuit, 1972.

Dugan, C. N. and Tracy B. Strong. "Music, Politics, Theater and Representation in Rousseau." In *Cambridge Companion to Rousseau.* Ed. Patrick Riley. Cambridge: Cambridge University Press, 2001, 329–64.

Eilenberg, Susan. *Strange Power of Speech. Wordsworth, Coleridge and Literary Possession,* New York: Oxford University Press, 1992.

Empson, William. "'Sense' in the *Prelude.*" In *The Structure of Complex Words.* Cambridge: Harvard University Press, 1989 [1st edn 1951], 289–305.

Florence, Penny. *Mallarmé, Manet and Redon: Visual and Aural Signs and the Generation of Meaning.* Cambridge: Cambridge University Press, 1986.

François, Anne-Lise. *Open Secrets. The Literature of Uncounted Experience.* Palo Alto, Ca.: Stanford, 2007.

Hartman, Geoffrey. *Wordsworth's Poetry. 1787–1814.* New Haven: Yale University Press, 1975.

Heffernan, James A. W. *Wordsworth's Theory of Poetry.* Ithaca: Cornell University Press, 1969.

Howe, Steven. *Heinrich von Kleist and Jean-Jacques Rousseau. Violence, Identity, Nation.* New York: Camden House, 2012.

Jacobus, Mary. *Tradition and Experiment in Wordsworth's Lyrical Ballads (1798).* Oxford: Clarendon Press, 1976.

Jameson, Frederic. *Valences of the Dialectic.* New York and London: New Left Review, 2009.

Jarvis, Simon. *Wordsworth's Philosophic Song.* Cambridge: Cambridge University Press, 2007.

Jones, John. *The Egotistical Sublime: A History of Wordsworth's Imagination.* London: Chatto & Windus, 1954.

Jones, Mark. *The 'Lucy Poems': A Case Study in Literary Knowledge.* Toronto: University of Toronto Press, 1995.

Kalar, Brent. *The Demands of Taste in Kant's Aesthetics.* London: Continuum, 2006.

Kulenkampff, Jan. *Kants Logik des aesthetischen Urteils.* Frankfurt: Klostermann, 1978.

Lavers, Anette, trans. Roland Barthes, *Mythologies.* New York: Farrar Strauss and Giroux, 1972.

Lindenberger Herbert. *On Wordsworth's Prelude.* Princeton: Princeton University Press, 1963.

Makkreel, Rudolf A. "Relating Kant's Theory of Reflective Judgment to the Law." *Washington University Jurisprudence Review* Vol. 6, No. 9 (2013): 147–160.

Marchant, Robert. *Principles of Wordsworth's Poetry.* Swansea: Brynmil Publishing Co., 1972.

Marken, Kenneth. *John Locke and English Literature of the Eighteenth Century.* New Haven: Yale University Press, 1936.

Morgenstern, Mira. *Rousseau and the Politics of Ambiguity.* University Park: The Penn State University Press, 1996.

Murray, Robert. N. *Wordsworth's Style. Figures and Themes in the Lyrical Ballads.* Lincoln: University of Nebraska Press, 1967.

Muth, Ludwig. *Kleist und Kant.* Köln: Kölner Universitätsverlag, 1954.

Owen, W. J. B. *Wordsworth as critic.* Toronto: University of Toronto Press, 1969.

Petscher, Iring. "Jean-Jacques Rousseau. Ethik und Politik." In *Rousseau und die Folgen.* Göttingen: Handerhoeck & Ruprecht, 1989, 1–23.

Rancière, Jacques. *Malaise dans l'ésthétique.* Paris: Galilée, 2004

Regier, Alexander. *Fracture and Fragmentation in British Romanticism.* (Cambridge: Cambridge University Press, 2010).

Reich, Klaus. *Rousseau und Kant.* Tübingen: Verlag J. C. B. Mohr, 1936.

Sheats, Paul D. *The Making of Wordsworth's Poetry.* Cambridge: Harvard University Press, 1973.

Smock, Ann, trans. Maurice Blanchot, *The Space of Literature.* Lincoln: University of Nebraska Press, 1982

Terada, Rei. *Feeling in Theory. Emotion after the "Death of the Subject."* Cambridge: Harvard University Press, 2001.

Vossler, Otto. *Rousseaus Freiheitslehre.* Göttingen: Vandenhoech & Ruprecht, 1962.

Weingart, Brigitte. "Contact at a Distance." In *Rethinking Emotion.* Ed. R. Campe and J. Weber. Berlin: de Gruyter, 2014, 73–100.

Wenzell, Christian Helmut. *Introduction to Kant's Aesthetics. Core Concepts and Problems.* London: Blackwell, 2005.

Wokler, Robert. *Rousseau, The Age of Enlightenment, and Their Legacies* (Princeton: Princeton University Press, 2012).

Wolfson, Susan. "Wordsworth's Craft." In *The Cambridge Companion to Wordsworth.* Ed. Stephen Gill. Cambridge: Cambridge University Press, 2003.

Wu, Duncan. *Wordsworth's Reading 1800–1815.* Cambridge: Cambridge University Press, 1998.

Zimmerman, Sarah. *Romanticism, Lyricism, and History.* Albany, NY: SUNY Press, 1999.

Index

meter, metrical and the geometrical 59–68, 59n, 70n, 90, 106; and "measured motion" of "mighty forms" acting "with purpose" of their own 52–3; Wordsworth's understanding of, as "something regular" 25–6, 31, 36–7, 39, 90, 94; dynamic scenographic and compositional linear use of 59, 61, 63, 67, 84, 86, 90–1, 94

Murray, Roger N. 72n

Nietzsche, Friedrich 112

originality (origin) conceived as creating "taste" by Wordsworth 34–6; defended in painting, by Mallarmé 35n; of "man" in Rousseau 113; of perception in relation to language, described by Rousseau 109–14

Pope, Alexander 14

Proust, Marcel 100, 119–20; and Hegel on the symbol 124–5, 127–8, 130, 132; involuntary corporal signs in, 101; on material semantics of Giotto's allegorical series of Vices and Virtues 120–5, 127–9, 133; "real horizon" in 98, 107–8, 129–33; on signal "invention" of "novelists" 107, 127, 129; on Swann's "ironic tone" 121, 121n

"purpose," poetic, as conceived by Wordsworth 4–6, 22–3, 29, 33–6, 43, 131–3, as "mode of meaning" exposed, according to Benjamin, in "death" of "original" by "translation" 81–2n; as nature's "own" 51–3, 90; of scenography in Wordsworth's verse 57, 59, 66–8, 70n, 77, 92, 104, 133; positive, of his *Critique*, as described by Kant 4n; "supersensory," of mind in experience of the "sublime," in Kant 10, 10–12; of travelers in *The Prelude* 79–81, 84, 88; n

Racine, Jean 100, 116

revolution, revolutions of language and society correlated by Wordsworth 9n, 18–19, 19n of "mode of thinking" ("Revolution der Denkart") described by Kant 18–19, 19n;

Rousseau, Jean-Jacques 34, 67, 100, 115, 118–19, 127, 130; *Discours sur l'origine et les fondements de l'inégalité parmi les hommes* (*Discourse on the origin and foundations of inequality among men*) 34n, 67n, 111–12; *Essai sur l'origine des langues* (*Essay on the Origin of Languages*) 108–14; *Lettre à d'Alembert* (Letter on Spectacles) 9n

scene, scenographic, scenography in the language theory of Rousseau 108–15, 119, 127, 130; in poetic practice of Wordsworth 22–3, 45–56, 59, 60, 63, 69, 74, 90–4, 104–6, 118, 131; in Wordsworth's poetic theory 7ff., 21–3, 25, 33, 36, 59, 59n, 60, 63, 69

Shakespeare, William 116

Shelley, P. B. 40n

sublime, the "and the Beautiful," by Wordsworth 12–13n; "antipathetic face of true goodness" in Proust 123; in Diderot's account of the actor 116–18; Kant's Analytic of 6, 10, 10n, 11–12, 11–13n, 37, 37n, 93, 93n, 109–10n; Wordsworth's poetics of 11–2, 23, 40, 83–5, 89–93; Wordsworth's theory of 7; and Kant's 10, 12, 70n.

temporality of sign production in Diderot 117–19, of development of language in Rousseau 111–14, 119; of understanding in Proust 121–3; cf. *difference*

visual field delimited by action in Wordsworth 62–3

www.ingramcontent.com/pod-product-compliance
Ingram Content Group UK Ltd.
Pitfield, Milton Keynes, MK11 3LW, UK
UKHW031251020325

455690UK00007B/104